SCHOOL LIBRARY STORYTIME

SCHOOL LIBRARY STORYTIME

JUST THE BASICS

Written and Illustrated by
Brenda S. Copeland and Patricia A. Messner

Just the Basics

 LIBRARIES UNLIMITED

AN IMPRINT OF ABC-CLIO, LLC
Santa Barbara, California • Denver, Colorado • Oxford, England

Library of Congress Cataloging-in-Publication Data

Copeland, Brenda S.
  School library storytime : just the basics / written and illustrated by Brenda S. Copeland and Patricia A. Messner.
    pages cm. — (Just the basics)
  Includes bibliographical references and index.
    ISBN 978-1-61069-202-1 (hardcopy) — ISBN 978-1-61069-203-8 (ebook) 1. Elementary school libraries—Activity programs—United States. 2. Storytelling—United States. 3. Children—Books and reading—United States. I. Messner, Patricia A. II. Title.
    Z675.S3C755 2013
    027.62′51—dc23   2013000170

ISBN: 978-1-61069-202-1
EISBN: 978-1-61069-203-8

17 16 15 14 13   1 2 3 4 5

This book is also available on the World Wide Web as an eBook.
Visit www.abc-clio.com for details.

Libraries Unlimited
An Imprint of ABC-CLIO, LLC

ABC-CLIO, LLC
130 Cremona Drive, P.O. Box 1911
Santa Barbara, California 93116-1911

This book is printed on acid-free paper ∞

Manufactured in the United States of America

CONTENTS

SERIES FOREWORD

School libraries are places to read, to explore, and to find information. When kindergarten students first visit a school library, they are told that this is the place where they will learn answers to their questions and that they will learn how to use the library to find those answers. And, as students grow and mature, the school library does indeed become that place for them, but we know that does not just happen. It takes a community, and that community is the library staff. The library staff must be knowledgeable, hardworking, and service oriented. They must possess a certain amount of basic information just to keep the library up and running.

Basic information is important information. It is often critical and in some cases not readily available. Running a school library well requires the assistance of several key individuals (library aides or clerks, volunteers, paraprofessionals, and technicians), in addition to the professional school librarian. Training these assistants to do the tasks required is time consuming, and often school librarians and district library coordinators have to construct their own training materials as well as do the one-on-one instruction at each library site.

In order to facilitate and help expedite this training, we offer this series of short, concise, and very practical books to aid in the training necessary to prepare assistants to help: organize, equip, and furnish a media center, manage a school library; prepare and circulate materials, and perform many other tasks that are necessary to the smooth operation of a school library today. The Just the Basics series is written by professionally trained and certified building-level school librarians working currently in the field. As we roll out this series, please let us know what you think. Do we need additional topics? Is the series usable in training situations? What comments do you have?

Please contact me at scoatney@abc-clio.com

SHARON COATNEY

Senior Acquisitions Editor
Libraries Unlimited
An Imprint of ABC-CLIO, LLC

INTRODUCTION

Library Store Hour is one of the most favorite extra activities primary grade students participate in during the school day. Teachers rejoice in the diversion of taking the students to the library for a story. Students enter with pent-up energy and wiggly bodies. Library staff stands at attention ready to wow the next group of young readers with picture books tucked under their arms. In the following pages, we hope to give some hints on how to make this time both manageable and exciting. This book contains a collection of stories and activities for use throughout the school year. Hopefully, they will be a spark for some very creative projects. Use these as written or spring off on your own. Remember, the youngest students in the school are excited about reading books. We want to harness this all-important natural resource. Even the oldest students will enjoy a good story if chosen carefully and presented well.

Probably the first and most asked question is *how do I read to students* and keep them hanging on to each page. Here are a few things to keep in mind.

1. *Read through the book ahead of time.* If the story is too complicated or the pictures do not lend themselves to being viewed in group setting, then lay aside and use another one. Some of the best stories also have complicated names for the main character. When you read through the text, if you stumble over the pronunciation, then you will do so during story time as well.

   Practice and, if it is still a problem, choose another story.

2. *Select stories that excite you.* Your excitement will carry over in your reading. Your voice inflections will help the students to be better readers themselves. If the main character looks like your pet, then play on that as you show the title and front cover. Help the students connect to the story. Let the fun and excitement carry the story line to the end. Give time at the end for students to share how the story made them feel or share connections to their own lives.

3. *Do not rush.* Stop often and talk about the illustrations and how they make the story more interesting. Ask key questions that help students predict what will happen on the next page. Build up the suspense and help them see the unexpected.

4. *Keep things simple.* Do not try to cover too much. Pick out one point and expand on it. Build on the concept all the way to the end. For example, if the story lends itself to story sequencing,

then concentrate on arranging the story in order. Have students recall those main events. This in itself is enough to cover with the reading.

5. *Pick stories that are suitable for the age-group.* Remember the very young need fewer words to a page. Older students can sit for a longer period of time and keep track of a more complex story line.

6. *Capitalize on repetitive phrases.* As you read, give these phrases to the students to watch or listen for and then read together. Stop and let them read those. They will catch on after the first couple of times. Especially, younger students enjoy watching for these and being able to recognize words. This will help with involving students and keeping them interested until the end of the story.

7. *Dress up.* Add a simple costume to your story time. A floppy hat or gardening apron can add excitement. It will bring smiles to young faces, and they will be wondering what you are up to during library time.

8. *Thumbs up.* Ask the students to listen for something during the story, and every time they hear it, they should give a thumbs-up sign. This should be a phrase that is repeated or anything that appears lots of times in the text. For example, if it is a counting story, the students should give a thumbs-up sign whenever they hear a number mentioned.

There are several ways *to hold a book* when reading to students. One way is to hold the book open and turn toward the students so all can view the pages as you read the text. This works well for short picture books and younger students. Students will need to be seated as close to you as possible and closer to each other so they can all see the pages at the same time. You need to be in a chair or a stool and slightly elevated. For an older audience, hold the book toward the reader, read the page, and then show the page to all before you turn the page. You can move the book around so all the audience can see the pages. This is probably the best technique for longer picture books and older students. Students can be seated in a story pit, tables, or close to the reader. Since you are reading the pages and then showing the pictures, students don't necessarily need to be really close to each other.

The *tone of voice* will make or break a read aloud. You will want students to be attentive, to be engaged, and to enjoy the story. After you have selected books to read to students, you will need to practice reading the books out loud. This helps you get the feel of the story, and if there are words you cannot pronounce, then you can look the words up in a dictionary. It also lets you hear your voice and how the story will sound to a group of students. Try to use expression with your voice and face as you read the story. If the story is exciting, read a little faster, and if the story is sad, read slower. Raise your voice if the character shouts, yells, screams, and so on. Lower your voice if the character whispers, mutters, hushes, and so on. Distinguish between male and female characters by the high or low pitch of your voice; also a young child or an older person would sound different.

Remember that practice makes perfect. You will soon learn what works for you and what style fits you. Do not be afraid to try something new. Also if a story does not go well with one group of students, do not feel bad if you change stories for the next group. Sometimes problems show up you cannot foresee. Students can get hung up on or upset about something that adults would not. If students say they already have heard the story, just tell them it is an old favorite and they will enjoy hearing it again. Solutions to these kind of situations come with practice.

Lastly, we have selected children's authors to celebrate each month in the library. These are located in the opening introduction to each month and listed along with their birthday. The chosen authors are ones that all students will recognize and hopefully will even have read some of their books. Create a birthday display with their books for students' free reading time or have books handy if needed to fill in time. Write the author's full name on a card to go with the display so students can better remember. We trust you will enjoy our collection of lessons. May many smiles and lots of laughter fill your library spaces.

1	2	3	4	5	6	7
8	9				13	14
15	16				20	21
22	23	24	25	26	27	28
29	30					

CHAPTER 1

SEPTEMBER

The last few days of August and the month of September are days and weeks of new beginnings. Kindergarteners are visiting a school library for the first time, and first and second graders are reviewing library procedures after three months of summer vacation. Expectations and procedures are a big part of the first library lessons so read alouds should be short and sweet. The following pages provide four lessons for each grade level, and the lessons and activities can be used for the first weeks of a new school year. Tomie dePaola and H. A. Rey are well-known children's authors and have birthdays in September, so you can celebrate these as well as the provided lessons. Tomie's is on September 15 and H. A.'s is on September 16.

KINDERGARTEN LESSONS

Lesson 1

Check It Out!: Reading, Finding, Helping

By Patricia Hubbell

Hubbell, Patricia. *Check It Out!: Reading, Finding, Helping.* Tarrytown, NY: Marshall Cavendish Children, 2011.

Summary: The librarian doesn't just read books to students; she makes the library special. She plans parties and knows how to look up lots of fun facts. Books and reading are her passion. This simple text takes the students on a journey through the library and introduces them to the job that the librarian does.

Skills: Library orientation

Grade Level: Kindergarten

Materials: Old library supply catalog
  Ten objects cut from a die-cut machine (the larger size works best)
  Marker, scissors, and glue

Instructions: Look for objects in the catalog that would represent the following: book cart, picture books, shelves, tables, chairs, computer, nonfiction books, library patron cards, checkout desk, and bulletin board. Cut them out and glue on to the die-cut pictures. With a marker, label the items so that the word appears under the picture. For example, the word "checkout desk" should appear under the picture of that item. Laminate if possible.

Lesson

1. Greet students and ask if someone knows what we do when we come to the library. Show the cover and point to the words as you read the title. Explain that we are going to read about the library.
2. Read the story slowly and stop to point out key things that appear in the pictures that are in a library. Example: book cart or computer.
3. After reading, share the picture cards one at a time. Point out that these were in the story and we are going to find them here in our library.
4. Walk the students through the library using the cards as your guide. At each stop, review what it is used for. Example: Picture book section: This is where you pick out a book to take home to read with your family.

Closure: Dismiss students to check out. Before the students return to class, review the cards again.

Lesson 2

Manners with a Library Book

By Amanda Doering Tourville

Tourville, Amanda Doering. *Manners with a Library Book*. Minneapolis: Picture Window Books, 2009.

Summary: Tia and Jaden take the reader through the steps of good book care. Starting with the checking out of the book, taking it home to enjoy, and then the returning of the book on time, this is an easy-to-follow helpful book for the youngest patrons. The book closes with some fun facts about libraries.

Skills: Book care

Grade Level: Kindergarten

Materials: Collection of damaged books
Poster paper and marker

Instructions: Pull an assortment of books that have been damaged by patrons. For example, torn pages, colored or drawn in books, chewed-up spines.

Lesson

1. Ask the students if they always remember to say please and thank you. Give time for students to respond. We call using words like this as "having good manners."
2. Stress that today's story is about good manners involving a library book. Give time to predict what that might mean.
3. Read the title and share the front cover.
4. As you read the story, stop and give students time to share or point out how they take care of the books they take home. Little ones always have things to share.

   Watch the time and cut short if time is a problem.

5. Share some of the damaged books that have been pulled ahead of time.

Closure: End the storytime by talking about ways to keep their library book safe. For example, keeping it in a book bag when you have finished reading the book. Or having a special place where the book is always kept like a top shelf in their bedroom. Make a list on the poster board. Dismiss students to check out.

Lesson 3

No T. Rex in the Library!

By Toni Buzzeo

Buzzeo, Toni. *No T. Rex in the Library!* New York: Margaret K. McElderry Books, 2010.

Summary: Tess is out of control in the library. Her mother tells her, she has to take a time-out and no beastie behavior in the library. T. Rex comes off the page in a book that Tess grabs. T. Rex zips, tilts, whirls, cannonballs, stomps, and reels through the library. He also trashes the shelves and rips books.

Skills: Proper behavior

Grade Level: Kindergarten

Materials: Behavior worksheet
No T. Rex Behavior in the Library Promise
Markers

Instructions: Enlarge the behavior worksheet so that all students can view. Attach it to an easel, wall, or end of a cabinet or book shelf.

Lesson

1. Introduce the title and author. Talk about the characters (Tess and T. Rex) on the cover.
2. Ask students to listen for how T. Rex acts in the story.
3. Read the story and share the pictures.
4. Ask the students to name some of the behaviors from the story.
5. Show the enlarged behavior worksheet and explain to the students, we will have to decide yes or no for each of the behaviors listed on the sheet.
6. Read through the behaviors one at a time and allow students to respond to each one of them.
7. Talk with students about the proper behavior in the library.

Closure: Allow time for the students to sign the No T. Rex Behavior in the Library Promise. Hang promise in the library for all patrons to view. Dismiss students to check out.

In the library we should:

1. _____ Stomp
   _____ Walk

2. _____ Talk loudly
   _____ Speak in a quiet voice

3. _____ Touch our classmates
   _____ Keep our hands and feet to ourselves

4. _____ Talk while the story is being read
   _____ Listen to the story

5. _____ Raise my hand when I want to talk
   _____ Talk without raising my hand

Our, No T. Rex Behavior in the Library, Promise!

Lesson 4

It's Library Day

By Janet Morgan Stoeke

Stoeke, Janet Morgan. *It's Library Day.* New York: Dutton Children's
   Books, 2008.

Summary: Several children anticipate the arrival of library day at
their school. They each are interested in different kinds of books. The
children meet Miss Faye, the new librarian, and she finds the perfect
book for each of the children. Miss Faye reads the children a story, and
they can't wait for the next library day.

Skills: Procedure for finding and checking out books

Grade Level: Kindergarten

Materials: Shelf markers and container
                List of steps to find and check out books

Instructions: Enlarge the five easy steps for finding and checking
out books or make your own.

Lesson

1. Introduce the title and author. Tell the students we are going to
   do the same thing the children in the story do.
2. Read the story and share the pictures.
3. Ask the following questions and call on students to answer.

   What was the librarian's name?
   How did Miss Faye help the children?
   Why was she able to help the children?
   What did the children do while waiting for Miss Faye to check
      out their books?

Closure: Show your shelf markers and explain the procedure for
finding books. Show the list of steps for finding and checking out
books. Display in a visible spot. Allow time for students to check out.

5 Easy Steps for Finding and Checking out Books!

```
┌─────────────────────────────────────────────┐
│                 Shelf Marker                  │
└─────────────────────────────────────────────┘
```

1.   Get a shelf marker from the container.

2.   Use the shelf marker to mark your spot.

3.   After finding your book, put the shelf marker away.

4.   Stand in line and wait your turn to check out your book at the desk.

Find a quiet place to read your book.

Stand in line here and wait your turn!

FIRST-GRADE LESSONS

Lesson 1

The Library Doors

By Toni Buzzeo

Buzzeo, Toni. *The Library Doors.* Fort Atkinson, WI: Upstart Books, 2008.

Summary: School Library activities portrayed in a repetitive text, set to the tune of "The Wheels on the Bus." Book includes a separate guide with the hand motions. Pictures are bright, colorful, and complete with extra words on the walls of the school. A fun engaging read aloud for young primary students.

Skills: Orientation to the layout of the library

Grade Level: First Grade

Materials: A copy of additional verses or write verses that apply to
        your situation
        Copies of the repetitive words

Instructions: Enlarge additional verses and the repetitive words on the copier, example might be 11 by 16, and one verse and one set of words to one piece of paper. Glue each verse on a separate piece of poster board and laminate.

Lesson

1. Place the repetitive words on an easel or chalk tray so that all students can view. Introduce the title of the book and author.
2. Use the separate guide for ideas or follow the lesson.
3. Tell students, they are going to sing the words to the book. Sing a verse of the familiar song "The Wheels on the Bus." Show the repetitive words and sing the first pages to the students. Ask students to sing with you the second time. Sing the words on the page while showing the pictures. You can have a student help you by showing the words as the each page is sung.
4. Be sure that you stop and read the extra words on the doors and walls. Students will ask if you forget.
5. After the story is completed, ask the following questions: Where did the children sit and listen to a story? What piece of equipment did the children use? What did the children use to hold their spot on the shelves? What did the librarian use to check out the books to the children?
6. Tell students, we do things a little different in this library. Show students the additional verses or write verses that apply to your situation. Move around the library and sing the additional verses and show students the library layout.

Closure: Students check out books to take home.

OPEN AND SHUT
COME AND GO
SHHH, SHHH, SHHH
COME, LET'S TALK
HEAR A TALE
LOOK FOR BOOKS
HOLD OUT SPOTS
READ, READ, READ

TICKETY, TICK
IN AND OUT
WAVE GOODBYE
COME AGAIN
WE'LL BE BACK

Optional Verses

We exit the storypit
ONE AT A TIME
ONE AT A TIME
ONE AT A TIME
We exit the story pit
ONE AT A TIME
So everyone is safe!

We checkout all kinds of book
EASY, FICTION, BIOGRAPHY
EASY, FICTION, BIOGRAPHY
EASY, FICTION, BIOGRAPHY
We checkout all kinds of book
EASY, FICTION, BIOGRAPHY
But don't forget Non Fiction!

We use paint sticks to
HOLD OUR SPOTS
HOLD OUR SPOTS
HOLD OUR SPOTS
We use paint sticks to
HOLD OUR SPOTS
Everyday in library!

We sit quietly and
READ OUR BOOKS
READ OUR BOOKS
READ OUR BOOKS
We sit quietly and
READ OUR BOOKS
Everyday in library!

Lesson 2

The Jellybeans and the Big Book Bonanza

By Laura Numeroff and Nate Evans

Numeroff, Laura and Nate Evans. *The Jellybeans and the Big Book Bonanza.* New York: Abrams Books for Young Readers, 2010.

Summary: Anna loves books and reads all the time. After reading her books, she always heads to the library to find new ones. When the class gets assigned a research book report, Anna takes her friends and introduces them to the librarian. They each find a book that is just right for them. When the day arrives to give the reports, Anna is afraid to read in front of the class. Her friends come to her rescue and help her out. This is a delightful introduction to the world of books and reading.

Skills: Library orientation for the different sections

Grade Level: First Grade

Materials: Collection of books about different subjects

Instructions: Pull books that include ones that Anna's friends picked out in the story (ballet, painting, and soccer). If possible, pick books that have lots of pictures and are easier for readers. Pull enough so that each student would have one to look through. Spread them out on tables or on an area of the floor that you can have students move to after the reading of the story.

Lesson

1. Share a nonfiction book that would represent what you like. If you like to draw or do art projects, pull one ahead of time and show it to the class. Explain that we are going to see how the characters in the story find that the library has all different types of books.
2. Read the story and share the pictures.
3. Ask the students questions about the book selection.

   Examples: Why did Emily pick a ballet book?
   Why did Bitsy choose a book about painters?
   Why did Nicole read a book about soccer?

4. Move to the tables or area where you have spread out the nonfiction titles. Ask the students to look through the books and decide which is their favorite.

Closure: First walk the students around the different sections of the library. Stress where the picture books are located. That would be like our story about the jellybeans. Second, point out where the nonfiction books are located. Those would be like the ballet or soccer books. Dismiss students to check out.

Lesson 3

LMNO Peas

By Keith Baker

Baker, Keith. *LMNO Peas.* New York: Beach Lane Books, 2010.

Summary: The alphabet peas are on the roll. These little green acrobats are rocking through the alphabet. They tumble and dance through the pages of this book as they introduce words that start with each letter.

Skills: Alphabetical order

Grade Level: First Grade

Materials: Collection of alphabet cards or make your own using construction paper that is cut in 3 by 5 inch blocks

Instructions: Cut the 3 by 5 inch cards using a paper cutter for easier cutting. Use a marker and mark the cards with letters of the alphabet. Make sure that only one letter appears on each card. Make them bold so students can read them when seated in a large group.

Lesson

1. Introduce the story by asking students to sing the alphabet song with you.
2. Show the front cover and read the title. Explain that we are making a trip through the alphabet.
3. Read the story.
4. After the reading, move through the alphabet cards asking what was the word that the author used for the letter A. Move through the cards. If the students cannot remember the words used in the story, ask if they can think of one that does.
5. Afterward, explain that we put the books on the shelves in the library according to the first letter of the author's last name. Show the front cover again and share the author's name. Keith Baker's book would be on the B shelf. Have a student go find the B shelf in the everybody/easy section.
6. If time permits, give each student a different letter and have them go find the shelf that matches their letter.

Closure: Line up students using the alphabet cards. Ask who has a last name that starts with the letter A. Move through the cards until everyone is in line to return to class. Dismiss students to check out.

Lesson 4

Dewey: There's a Cat in the Library!

By Vicki Myron and Bret Witter

Myron, Vicki and Bret Witter. *Dewey: There's a Cat in the Library!* New York: Little, Brown and Company, 2009.

Summary: A stray kitten is left in the book drop at the library in Spencer, Iowa. Vicki the librarian decides to clean him up and give him a name. The kitten becomes Dewey Readmore Books. He makes friends with all the patrons, even the most difficult ones. He makes even the saddest little girl smile.

Skills: Library spine labels

Grade Level: First Grade

Materials: Picture spine labels that are used in your library (cats, dogs, horses)
4 by 6 inch cards cut from construction paper

Instructions: Cut the cards from construction paper using the paper cutter. Cut one for each of the spine labels that you wish to share with the students. Most elementary school libraries label favorites that kids always ask for. For example, cats, dogs, and horses. Mount one sticker to each card and laminate.

Lesson

1. Share the book with the students. The reading of this story never fails to delight the audience. They will want to share many cat stories from their own experiences. Gage your time when it comes to sharing. This is a popular topic, so many will want to talk.
2. Point out that this book has a spine label that helps us find cat books. Show the cat sticker on the spine.
3. Remind students that the spine of a book is super important. Just like our spines help hold us up, the book spine helps hold the pages together. It faces out on the shelf, so we can find the books more easily. Model this for the students.
4. Share the cards that have been prepared ahead of time.

Closure: Give cards to groups of kids and have them find books with those labels. If time permits, you can ask them to count how many they find. If time is short, then they can go stand by the shelf where they have located one of the stickers. Ask students to return to the story area. Collect cards and ask groups to report how many of that kind of book did they find. Dismiss students to check out. Before returning to class, ask if any one checked out a book with a spine label.

SECOND-GRADE LESSONS

Lesson 1

Library Lion

By Michelle Knudsen

Knudsen, Michelle. *Library Lion.* Cambridge, MA: Candlewick Press, 2006.

Summary: A lion comes to the library and makes himself at home, sniffs the card catalog, rubs his head on the new book collection, and falls asleep in the story corner. The lion roars after storytime is over, and the librarian tells him, he has to leave if he is not quiet. The lion makes himself useful and visits the library every day and enjoys story-time. The librarian falls and hurts her arm and can't get up. She sends the lion to get help.

Skills: Review of proper behavior and the three parts of a story

Grade Level: Second Grade

Materials: A copy of your rules; see example at the end of this lesson

Lesson

1. Talk to the students about the three parts of a story: beginning, middle, and end.
2. Introduce the title and author and ask students to listen for the three parts and be ready to share when the story is finished.
3. Read the story and share the pictures.
4. Allow time for the students to respond with the three parts of the story. The beginning might be the lion came to the library, made himself at home, and his behavior was not good. The middle of the story is the lion helping at the library and waiting for storytime to begin. The end of the story is when the lion has to help the librarian, and he gets too loud and leaves the library because he thinks he is kicked out of the library.

Closure: Briefly talk about the rules of your library, reminding students of all the fun activities taking place in the library and the need for them to be on their best behavior. Show the rules that you have posted in the library. Dismiss students to check out.

GRRRRRRRRRRRRROar!

Don't Be a Lion in the Library!

Always remember to:

1. Speak in a quiet voice.

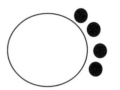

2. Walk

3. Listen to your friends and the teacher.

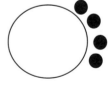

Lesson 2

Too Much Noise in the Library

By Susan Margaret Chapman

Chapman, Susan Margaret. *Too Much Noise in the Library*. Janesville, WI: Upstart Books, 2010.

Summary: Ms. Reade, the librarian, runs a lively media center with lots of library noises like keyboards clicking and pages rustling. The mayor of the town loves libraries because they are so quiet. With the help of the students, he learns that libraries have joyful noises.

Skills: Library behavior

Grade Level: Second Grade

Materials: Chart paper and black marker

Instructions: Before the arrival of the students, make a large T on the chart paper. A T chart is a helpful way to display two different views about a subject. In this case, you want to talk about the good noise and the bad noise in a library.

Lesson

1. Read the title and share the front cover of the book. Ask if the title gives us a hint as to what this story is about. Give time for comments.
2. Read the story, and as the class catches on to the sound effects that are mentioned in the text, they can do the sounds. For example, kerplop kerplop, clickety click, zippedy zing, blabbety blab, rustle rustle, yackety yack, hee hee.

   These seven phrases are repeated through the book, and the students will enjoy reading these as a group.
3. Ask the students: Do we need happy noises sometimes in the library? What were the happy noises in the story?
4. Using the T chart, guide the students in making a list of good and bad noises in the library.

Closure: After book selection, return to the large group and ask if they heard good or bad noises in the library. Review rules that you have in place as a way of reinforcing the needed behavior in the library.

Lesson 3

Penelope Popper Book Doctor

By Toni Buzzeo

Buzzeo, Toni. *Penelope Popper Book Doctor.* Madison, WI: Upstartbooks, 2011.

Summary: Penelope Popper wants to be a doctor. She has all the necessities: a bag, a coat, and a badge. Penelope tries to check everyone's blood pressure, reflexes, and heartbeat. She is sent to the library to see if Ms. Brisco can find something for her to do. Penelope becomes interested in helping hurting books. She becomes Dr. Penelope Popper, book doctor.

Skills: Proper book care

Grade Level: Second Grade

Materials: Poster board
Markers
Box or wrapper from a bar of soap
Glove
Stuffing
A small triangular piece of paper
Empty soda can
Shelf marker
Glue and tape
Printer labels 2 by 4 inches

Instructions: Make a book care rules poster using the poster board and markers. Use the five rules from the book or modify for your library. Glue the empty soap box or package by the rule on keeping your hands clean. Stuff the glove with stuffing and glue next to the rule on turning the pages at the upper right-hand corner. Glue the triangular paper next to the rule about dog earring pages. Turn the one side of the triangle under about half an inch and tape down the turned underside so it looks like a page has been turned down. Glue the empty soda can next to the rule about keeping books safe from liquids. Glue a shelf marker next to the rule about using a shelf marker to hold your spot. Print honorary book doctor name tags for students who find damaged books. See name tag labels at the end of this lesson.

Lesson

1. Introduce the title and author. Ask students if they have any ideas of what this book would be about. Let students share their ideas.
2. Ask students to listen for five book care rules.

3. Read the story and share the pictures.
4. Allow time for students to share the five book care rules.

Closure: Show students the book care rules and review. Tell students that if they find a book that needs care, they should please let the staff know. The staff will give the student an honorary book doctor name tag to wear that day. Hang the book care rules in a visible spot. Dismiss students to check out.

Dr._____

Book

Doctor

Dr._____

Book

Doctor

Dr._____

Book

Doctor

Dr._____

Book

Doctor

Dr._____

Book

Doctor

Dr._____

Book

Doctor

Dr._____

Book

Doctor

Dr._____

Book

Doctor

Lesson 4

The Best Book to Read

By Debbie Bertram and Susan Bloom

Bertram, Debbie and Susan Bloom. *The Best Book to Read.* New York: Random House, 2008.

Summary: Students ride the bus to the public library and the librarian shows them all the different kinds of books. She helps each one of them find just the right book.

Skills: Call numbers for the four sections of the library—Easy, Fiction, Biography, and Nonfiction

Grade Level: Second Grade

Materials: Black marker
          Index cards
          A black top hat
          A book to represent each section of the library

Instructions: Using the examples provided, write call numbers on index cards. Laminate for long wear. Place the index card spine labels in the top hat. Print the names of the four sections of the library on large pieces of paper.

Lesson

1. Introduce the title and author. Tell students to listen for the many different kinds of books in the library. Examples: space books, fairy tales, and so on.
2. Read the story and share the pictures.
3. Allow time for students to recall the different kinds of books mentioned in the library.
4. Show the titles of the four sections of the library. Stand them in a chalk tray or on the floor in front of the students. Talk about the sections and show the examples along with the call numbers. Discuss the call numbers and the difference in the four sections.
5. Bring the top hat out. Students will take turns pulling a call number out of the hat and matching it up with the title of the correct section of the library.

Closure: Remind students, the library is a magical place. You can go anywhere and be anything when you read a book. Students explore the magic in the library and check out books.

E CAR	E SEU	E WOO	E BRI	E BRO
FIC BAG	FIC ROW	FIC ROY	FIC KLI	FIC PAR
B WAS	B TUB	B FRA	B AAR	B LIN
E COL	E FLE	E WIL	FIC CHR	FIC HAD
B JEF	B MAD	B JOR	B ADA	B WRI

598	220	636	743	030
CAR	SEU	WOO	BRI	BRO
818	917	796	623	398
BAG	ROW	ROY	KLI	PAR
507	394	567	574	597
WAS	TUB	FRA	AAR	LIN
629	745	641	910	912
COL	FLE	WIL	CHR	HAD
999	100	358	591	599
JEF	MAD	JOR	ADA	WRI

Biography

Everybody/Easy

Fiction

Biography

RESOURCES

Kindergarten

Buzzeo, Toni. *Adventure Annie Goes to Kindergarten.* New York: Dial Books for Young Readers, 2010.

Dewdney, Anna. *Llama Llama Misses Mama.* New York: Viking, 2009.

Kroll, Virginia. *On the Way to Kindergarten.* New York: Puffin Books, 2006.

Lakin, Patricia. *Max & Mo's First Day at School.* New York: Aladdin, 2007.

Shea, Bob. *Dinosaur vs. the Library.* New York: Hyperion Books, 2011.

Sierra, Judy. *Born to Read.* New York: Knopf, 2007.

First Grade

Bunting, Eve. *Our Library.* New York: Clarion Books, 2008.

Hills, Tad. *How Rocket Learned to Read.* New York: Schwartz & Wade Books, 2010.

Klein, Adria F. *Tia Tape Measure.* Mankoto, MN: Stone Arch Books, 2012.

Koontz, Robin. *The Case of the Shifting Stacks.* Edna, MN: Abdo Consulting Group, Inc., 2010.

Stadler, Alexander. *Beverly Billingsly Borrows a Book.* New York: Harcourt, Inc., 2002.

Second Grade

Dannenberg, Julie. *First Day Jitters.* Watertown, MA: Charlesbridge, 2000.

Henson, Heather. *That Book Woman.* New York: Atheneuin Books for Young Readers, 2008.

Lies, Brian. *Bats at the Library.* Boston: Houghton Mifflin Co., 2008.

Shields, Gillian. *Library Lily.* Grand Rapids, MI: Eerdmans Books for Young Readers, 2011.

Sierra, Judy. *Mind Your Manners, B.B. Wolf.* New York: Knopf, 2008.

Willis, Joanne. *Delilah D. at the Library.* New York: Clarion Books, 2006.

		1	2	3	4	5
6	7				11	12
13	14				18	19
20	21				25	26
27	28	29	30			

CHAPTER 2

OCTOBER

October has several special weeks and days: Columbus Day, National Fire Prevention Week, and Halloween. Several schools are choosing to not celebrate Halloween and are replacing that holiday with fall or harvest parties. We did not include Halloween lessons in this chapter, but we found a few Halloween books for the resource page. Celebrate author David Shannon's birthday this month on October 5.

FIRE PREVENTION WEEK LESSONS

Lesson 1

This Is the Firefighter

By Laura Godwin

Godwin, Laura. *This Is the Firefighter.* New York: Hyperion Books, 2009.

Summary: This book takes the reader from a fire call through to the rescue. Simple text and pictures introduce young students to the fire station and the equipment needed to fight a fire and emphasize the importance of firefighters to the community.

Skills: Introduce a fire drill in the library

Grade Level: Kindergarten

Materials: Plastic fire hat, boots, and black coat

Lesson

1. Wear the fire hat and other costume as you greet the students. Ask if they can guess what the story will be about. Allow time for students to respond. Inform students that the second week in October is Fire Prevention Week, and the reason for this week is to help everyone remember to be safe with fire and not play with matches and other dangerous things.
2. Most schools will have had a school-wide fire drill by the first week in October, so help students remember the fire drill the school had in September. Go over the procedure and where to line up in the library.
3. Introduce the title and author and tell the students, this story is about a real fire and how the firefighters fight the fire and rescue the people.
4. Read the story and share the pictures.
5. Discuss the story and what the waiting people did while the firefighters were rescuing the other people. Talk about the word "hero" using simple words like a hero is an important helper to people, reinforcing the importance of being quiet during a fire drill and following directions.
6. Visit www.firepreventionweek.org for other ideas.

Closure: Practice lining up and even walking outside if possible. Dismiss students to check out.

Lesson 1

Firefighters! Speeding! Spraying! Saving!

By Patricia Hubbell

Hubbell, Patricia. *Firefighters! Speeding! Spraying! Saving!* Tarrytown, NY: Marshall Cavendish, 2007.

Summary: A rhyming story with many fire and firefighter-related words. The story takes the reader from a fire call to the exhausted firefighters finally resting. This story is a fun read aloud filled with sound words that are fun to read and listen to.

Skills: Review of fire drills

Grade Level: First Grade

Materials: Fire drill procedure

Lesson

1. Ask the students what they think of when they hear the word "firefighter." Allow time for several students to respond. If you have a wipe-off or chart paper, make a list as the students respond.
2. Introduce the title and author and tell the students to listen for other words to add to the list.
3. Share the story and pictures.
4. Add additional words to the list. Talk about the hard work and dedication of firefighters. Ask the question: How can we help firefighters? Allow time for students to respond. Talk about the importance of being safe and following directions when we have a fire drill.

Closure: Review the fire drill procedure for the library. Dismiss students to check out.

Lesson 1

Spark the Firefighter

By Stephen Krensky

Krensky, Stephen. *Spark the Firefighter.* New York: Dutton Children's Books, 2008.

Summary: Spark is a dragon who doesn't like fire. He volunteers as a firefighter to overcome his fears. Spark trains, practices, and finally overcomes his fears and is able to fight fires. He learns to shoot flames to fight a fire in a barn and saves the animals. This is a fiction story but has many facts about the hard work firefighters do each day.

Skills: Reinforce the importance of firefighters

Grade: Second Grade

Materials: Card stock
              Markers
              Pencils
              Crayons

Lesson

1. Ask students the question: What do firefighters do all day? Allow time for two or three students to answer.
2. Introduce the title and author and tell students to listen for additional activities in which firefighters engage.
3. Share the story and pictures. Discuss with the students other activities of firefighters. Lead the students into a discussion of the importance of firefighters.

Closure: Students make cards for local firefighters. Dismiss students to check out.

COLUMBUS DAY LESSONS

Lesson 2

Columbus Day

By Robin Nelson

Nelson, Robin. *Columbus Day.* Minneapolis: Lerner Publications, 2010.

Summary: This is an easy introduction to Christopher Columbus with pictures and large print. The basics are covered with the younger patrons in mind. A simple time line is included in the back for easy reference.

Skills: Holiday celebration—Columbus Day

Grade Level: Kindergarten

Materials: Construction paper cut in strips about 4 by 10 inches
Black marker

Instructions: Using the glossary at the back of the book, print words that might not be familiar to the kindergarteners such as "celebrate" and "explorer." As you read through the text, others might stand out as ones that also may need to be discussed. Keep to six or less since it is hard for kindergarten students to keep track of too many concepts at one time.

Lesson

1. Greet students and ask: What holiday is celebrated in October? Give time for the class to respond. If the classroom teacher has introduced Columbus Day, then students will volunteer, and if not, you may need to give them some prompts and/or introduce the holiday yourself.
2. Share the book and front cover explaining that the book is a fact book about this holiday. A fact book has lots of interesting information about a subject.
3. Read the book stopping to talk about the pages and events as you go along. For example, one picture has a float decorated to look like a boat and someone dressed as Christopher Columbus riding on it in a parade. This would be a good time to stress that sometimes we celebrate with parades or parties. The students will probably have their own experiences to add to that discussion.
4. After reading, share the word "cards" and go over the words asking students to explain what each means. Correct any mistakes. Remember to keep the answers simple. Monitor the discussion time by the interest of students.

Closure: Dismiss students to select library books. Tell them to be explorers and find new and interesting books to take home to read with their families.

Lesson 2

Columbus Day

By Molly Aloian

Aloian, Molly. *Columbus Day*. New York: Crabtree, 2010.

Summary: This is a kid-friendly book that helps students understand the celebration of Columbus Day. This book includes historical background as well as modern ways to commemorate the founding of America.

Skills: Holiday celebration—Columbus Day

Grade Level: First Grade

Materials: Poster board
            Marker

Instructions: Copy the rhyme found on page 25 of the text onto the poster board. Make it large enough for the students to read as a group. Decorate with pictures if available. Also check out activities listed in the back for possible projects that could be included in the story hour.

Lesson

1. Greet students and ask: What holiday is celebrated in October? Give time for class to respond. If the classroom teacher has introduced Columbus Day, then students will volunteer. If not, you may have to introduce the holiday to the students.
2. Share the book and front cover explaining that the book is a fact book about Christopher Columbus and the discovery of America.
3. Read the book stopping to talk about the pages and events as you go along. The students might be interested in the foods that the crew might have eaten.
4. Bring out the poster and read the rhyme to the class. If time allows, let the students read and chant the rhyme. Divide and let girls read the rhyme and then let the boys read the text.

Closure: Some optional activities are listed in the back of the book. Choose one that is appropriate for the age-group you are teaching. For example, mapping the voyage: guide students through the route of the voyage using a world atlas or large wall map. One student can hold one end of the length of string at the beginning point and another student can hold the other end of the string at the point of arrival in the new world. Dismiss students to check out.

Lesson 2

You Wouldn't Want to Sail with Christopher Columbus!

By Fiona Macdonald

Macdonald, Fiona. *You Wouldn't Want to Sail with Christopher Columbus!*
New York: Franklin Watts, 2009.

Summary: This is an interesting overview of the difficulties of the
voyage of Christopher Columbus complete with cartoons characters
that make the text more appealing to the younger reader. It is packed
with lots of facts and interesting trivia.

Skills: Holiday celebration—Columbus Day

Grade Level: Second Grade

Materials: Drawing paper
Crayons
Pencils

Instructions: Cut paper into half sheets using 8-1/2 by 11 inch
construction paper or drawing paper.

Lesson

1. Welcome students to the library and share the title and author
of the book. Review with the students the job of each and explain that both the author and the illustrator of this book did an
interesting job of sharing the facts with the reader.
2. Pick sections of each page to read to the students. Some groups
will find it long while others will enjoy looking for the cartoons
and extra facts. Monitor the students' level of interest and ad-
just the time needed to complete both the reading and the
activity.
3. Let the students vote on whether they would have liked to have
been on the voyage. Ask them to justify their answer. For example, most ships have lots of rats. Most students will enjoy
pointing out the gross things that they learned. Limit comments to a few of the students so they will have time to draw
and write out their reasons. If students have trouble with a
complete sentence, then they could limit it to one or two words.
Example: rats.

Closure: Give out paper and have students draw their own cartoon
character with the attached fact that they learned from the reading.
Collect and display on a bulletin board with the title as the heading for
the display. Dismiss students to check out.

FALL LESSONS

Lesson 3

There Was an Old Lady Who Swallowed Some Leaves!

By Lucille Colandro

Colandro, Lucille. *There Was an Old Lady Who Swallowed Some Leaves!* New York: Scholastic Inc. 2010.

Summary: A fun fall book that has a singsong cadence. As the old lady swallows each item, the students will realize that it is a scarecrow that comes out when she sneezes.

Skills: Sequencing

Grade Level: Kindergarten

Materials: Seven pieces of construction paper 8-1/2 by 11 inches
Pictures or cutouts of leaves, shirt, pumpkin, pole, pants, rope, and some hay
Glue, scissors, and marker
Drawing paper and crayons for each student

Instructions: Glue a picture on each sheet of the construction paper. Label each picture with the name of what it is. For example, the word "leaves" should be written under the picture of the leaves.

Lesson

1. Share the front cover of the book, reading the title and author.
2. Since several books are similar to this one, students may recognize this and wish to share. Give time for this to happen. It is important for students to connect to other stories that they have heard. Here are a few examples.

Colandro, Lucille. *There Was an Old Lady Who Swallowed a Chick.* New York: Scholastic, 2009.

Colandro, Lucille. *There Was an Old Lady Who Swallowed a Bat.* New York: Scholastic, 2002.

Colandro, Lucille. *There Was an Old lady Who Swallowed a Shell.* New York: Scholastic, 2008.

Taback, Simms. *There Was an Old Lady Who Swallowed a Fly.* New York: Viking, 1997.

3. Read the book stopping often to predict what the old lady might swallow next.
4. After the reading, spread out the pictures in the wrong order.
5. Rotate around the group asking what happened next in the story.

6. Read the book a second time to check to see if the students remember the order.

Closure: Give students paper and crayons and ask them to draw the scarecrow in the story. Let them pair up with a partner at the end to see if all seven items are in their picture. Dismiss students to check out.

Lesson 3

Leaf Trouble

By Jonathan Emmett

Emmett, Jonathan. *Leaf Trouble.* New York: Chicken House: 2009.

Summary: Pip, the squirrel, experiences falling leaves and thinks that something is wrong with the trees. He enlists his sister, Blossom, to help him attach the leaves back on the trees. Finally, his mother explains that the trees need to rest and new leaves will form again in the spring.

Skills: Characters and setting

Grade Level: First Grade

Materials: Fall colors of construction paper (yellow, red, and orange)
Die-cut machine and die of a leaf or leaf pattern
Marker
Two pieces of 8-1/2 by 11 card stock
Small garbage bag

Instructions: Cut out lots of leaves from the die-cut machine or a leaf pattern. Write the characters on the leaves, one character per leaf. Also write action words on some of the leaves, like sniffed, scampered, and skittered. Write words that describes the setting or items that might be in the setting. Example: forest, fall, outside, trees, leaves, sun, branches. Write the words "characters" and "setting" on the card stock. Cut extra leaves for two piles of leaves. Place the leaves with the words in the small garbage bag.

Lesson

1. Introduce the words "characters" and "setting" using the word cards made from the card stock. This might be a review lesson for some, so ask the students to help.
2. Introduce the title and author and ask students to listen for the characters and setting. Also ask students to listen for any words that might describe or relate to the characters and setting.
3. Read and share the pictures.
4. On the floor in front of the students, make two piles of leaves with the extra leaves. Place the word cards under the piles. One pile will be for the character and the other will be for the setting.
5. Have the students draw out a leaf and read what is printed on the leaf. First grade may need help reading some words, so offer assistance if need be. The student will need to decide which pile their leaf belongs in.

Closure: Dismiss students to check out.

Amelia Bedelia's First Apple Pie

By Herman Parish

Parish, Herman. *Amelia Bedelia's First Apple Pie.* New York: Greenwillow Books, 2010.

Summary: Amelia likes everything about the fall of the year including picking apples and making pies. Grandma shows her how to roll out the pie crust and get the apples ready. She even makes a small one all by herself.

Skills: Author, title, and publisher
Sequencing

Grade Level: Second Grade

Materials: Paper copy of the apple pattern
Crayons
pencils

Instructions: Run copies of the apple pattern for each child. Collect pencils and crayons as well.

Lesson

1. Read the title and share the front cover of the book. Talk about the job of the author as well as the publisher. Share with the class that this information can be found on the title page of the book. Publisher is usually listed on the bottom of the title page. Title is always in big letters.

2. Read the story to the class. Stop often to explain how Amelia gets words mixed up. She always sees things differently. It takes a little while for students to see this pattern. They will need help with this at the beginning of the story. As the story progresses, they are able to point them out and explain them better.

3. Review with the class what steps Amelia took for making the pie. These should include picking the apples, cutting up the apples, finding the pan, rolling out the crust, and filling the pie shell.

4. Give the students each a copy of the apple pattern. Explain that they are going to write the five steps that Amelia took to make the apple pie. These might be best if students use only one word. For example, pick, cut, pan, crust, and fill the shell. If students struggle, then write these on the board for them. When they have completed the written part, they can color their apple.

Closure: Go back to the page of the different kinds of apples in the text, and let students decide what is their favorite kind. Some will be familiar, and others might be ones that they have not heard of before. Dismiss students to check out.

PUMPKIN LESSONS

Lesson 4

Pumpkins

By Robin Nelson

Nelson, Robin. *Pumpkins*. Minneapolis: Lerner, 2009.

Summary: Colorful pictures and simple text describe the life cycle of a pumpkin. The younger reader is introduced to pumpkin facts as well as a diagram of the growing process.

Skills: Sequencing

Grade Level: Kindergarten

Materials: Six pieces of orange construction paper
Marker

Instructions: Using the pattern of the pumpkin provided in the text, cut out six from the orange construction paper. Draw pictures using the book as a guide that would represent the six stages of the cycle of a pumpkin. For example, seed, sprout, seeding, vines, small green pumpkin, and the full-grown pumpkin.

Lesson

1. Share the title page of the book and point out the title and author. Explain that this is a fact book or nonfiction book about how pumpkins grow to be big enough to carve for Halloween.
2. Read the text stopping often to explain the pictures.
3. Ask questions as you move through the book. For example, How many of you have gone to a farm to pick a pumpkin growing in the field? What color was it? What sizes did you see?
4. Review the cycle drawing on page 18. The diagram shows the steps.

Closure: Mix up the pumpkins that have been prepared ahead of time. Lay them out in front of the students. Explain the pictures are in the wrong order. What does the farmer plant? That would be number one. Lay out that picture in a separate row. Ask what happens to the seed? Give a student the opportunity to come up and place the sprout next to the seed. Proceed until all the steps are in the correct order. Dismiss students to check out.

Lesson 4

Pick a Perfect Pumpkin

By Robin Koontz

Koontz, Robin. *Pick a Perfect Pumpkin.* Mankato, MN: Picture Window Books, 2011.

Summary: Children visit the pumpkin farm, learn how pumpkins grow, and learn about many uses for pumpkins and that pumpkins come in a variety of colors. The children also pick pumpkins to take home and carve. A good nonfiction read aloud.

Skills: Reinforce title and author
Introduce illustrator and illustrations

Grade Level: First Grade

Materials: Four brown grocery bags
One lunch bag
Orange construction paper
Black marker
Pictures of pencils, paint brushes, and markers
Illustrations from magazines or books that are being discarded
Card stock

Instructions: Copy and cut out the pumpkin pattern. Trace and cut out 23 pumpkins from the orange construction paper. Using the marker, write the words "title," "author," "illustrator," and "illustrations" on four different pumpkins. Laminate for longer wear. Tape the four pumpkins to the four brown paper bags. Write four well-known authors' names on four of the pumpkins. Write four well-known titles on four of the pumpkins. Examples might be: *Fancy Nancy, Where the Wild things Are, The Cat in the Hat,* and *The Polar Express.*

Tape pictures of pencils, paintbrushes, and markers on three of the pumpkins. Tape illustrations from magazines or books on four of the pumpkins. Laminate all the pumpkins. Place the pumpkins in the lunch bag. Make word cards by writing the words, "author," "title," "illustrator," and "illustrations" on the card stock.

Lesson

1. Introduce the title and author of the book. Review the meaning of the title and author. Show the word cards as you talk about the title and the author.
2. Read the story and talk about the pictures.
3. Introduce the words "illustrations" and "illustrator" using the word cards. Discuss what tools an illustrator might use to create pictures for books.

4. Show the bags with the pumpkins on the front and set them in front of the class.
5. Have the students draw out a pumpkin out of the lunch bag, tell the class what it is, and add it to the appropriate bag.

Closure: Dismiss students to check out books.

Lesson 4

How Many Seeds in a Pumpkin?

By Margaret McNamara

McNamara, Margaret. *How Many Seeds in a Pumpkin?* New York: Schwartz & Wade Books, 2007.

Summary: A classroom explores how many seeds there are in three different-size pumpkins. Students estimate the amount of seeds, dig seeds out of pumpkins, and count the seeds. Surprising results are revealed after students count the seeds. Interesting facts about pumpkins are also included in this fun math-related book.

Skills: Beginning, middle, and end of a story

Grade Level: Second Grade

Materials: Four brown grocery bags
Orange construction paper
Black marker
Pumpkin pattern

Instructions: Using the pumpkin pattern, cut 25 pumpkins from the orange paper. Write the title and author on one. Write the words "beginning," "middle," and "end" on three other pumpkins. Laminate and tape each of these pumpkins on a brown bag, so you should have four bags that are labeled. With the other pumpkins, write the individual events in the story on each of the pumpkins. Laminate and place the pumpkins with the events on the bag with the author and title.

Lesson

1. Display bags for the class to view during the reading of the story.
2. Introduce the title and author.
3. Tell the students that every story has a beginning, middle, and end. Listen for the events in the story, and afterward, we will decide which events belong in the beginning, middle, and end.
4. Read and share the pictures.
5. Let students draw out the pumpkins with the events written on them that are in the brown bag with the title and author. Have the students read the event and place in the correct bag the beginning, middle, and end. Make corrections as needed.

Closure: Dismiss students to check out.

42   From *School Library Storytime: Just the Basics* written and illustrated by Brenda S. Copeland and Patricia A. Messner. Santa Barbara, CA: Libraries Unlimited. Copyright © 2013.

From *School Library Storytime: Just the Basics* written and illustrated by Brenda S. Copeland and Patricia A. Messner. Santa Barbara, CA: Libraries Unlimited. Copyright © 2013.

RESOURCES

Fire

Aloian, Molly. *Fire Trucks Racing to the Scene.* New York: Crabtree, 2011.

Bodden, Valerie. *Fire Trucks.* Mankato, MN: Creative Education, 2011.

Butler, Dori Hillestand. *F Is for Firefighting.* Gretna, LA: Pelican, 2007.

Coppendale, Jean. *Fire Trucks and Rescue Vehicles.* Buffalo, NY: Firefly Books, 2010.

Mayer, Mercer. *Going to the Firehouse.* New York: HarperCollins, 2008.

Columbus Day

Craats, Rennay. *Columbus Day.* New York: AV^2, 2011.

Fall

Anderson, Shelia. *Are You Ready for Fall?* Minneapolis: Lerner Publications, 2010.

Ballard, Lisa. *Busy Animals: Learning about Animals in Autumn.* Mankato, MN: Picture Window Books, 2011.

Harris, Calvin. *Scarecrows.* Mankato, MN: Capstone Press, 2008.

Iwamura, Kazuo. *Hooray for Fall!* New York: NorthSouth, 2009.

Knootz, Robin. *Apples, Apples Everywhere! Learning about Apple Harvests.* Mankato, MN: Picture Window Books, 2011.

Nelson, Robin. *Pumpkins.* Minneapolis: Lerner, 2009.

Rawlinson, Julia. *Fletcher and the Falling leaves.* New York: Greenwillow Books, 2008.

Rustad, Martha E. H. *Animals in Fall.* Mankato, MN: Capstone Press, 2008.

Rustad, Martha E. H. *Leaves in Fall.* Mankato, MN: Capstone Press, 2008.

Yolen, Jane. *The Scarecrow's Dance.* New York: Simon & Schuster, 2009.

Halloween

De Las Casas, Dianne. *The House That Witchy Built.* Gretna, LA: Pelican Publishing Company, 2011.

Fraser, Mary Ann. *Heebie-Jeebie Jamboree.* Honesdale, PA: Boyds Mills Press, 2011.

Rohmann, Eric. *Bone Dog.* New York: Roaring Brook Press, 2011.

					1	2
3	4				8	9
10	11				15	16
17	18	19	20	21	22	23
24	25	26	27	28	29	30

CHAPTER 3

NOVEMBER

November is full of holidays and specials days the library can celebrate; Election Day, Veterans Day, and Thanksgiving are the three we highlight in these lessons. The library can also celebrate authors' birthdays: examples might be Kevin Henkes, Stephanie Calmenson, and Lois Ehlert. We have included these authors' newest books in the resource page.

ELECTION DAY LESSONS

The presidential election brings just as much excitement to the elementary school as any other place in the United States. School programs and studies also focus on state and local governments and elections at those levels. In our selections, here we have chosen a nonfiction book to read to each grade level as a way of introduction to elections and the process of deciding on our leaders. One way to also enrich this time is to let the students vote on favorite authors or books. By doing this in conjunction with the election, the students can better understand the process. Keep things simple by selecting books or authors that the younger students are already familiar with such as Dr. Seuss and Marc Brown. Pull lots of books by both the authors and create a display. Read several at this time as well, and let students illustrate their favorite book covers. Voting can then take place during library time around Election Day. Post the results on a bulletin board.

Lesson 1

Let's Vote on It!

By Janice Behrens

Behrens, Janice. *Let's Vote on It!* New York: Children's Press, 2010.

Summary: This is an easy to follow explanation of the election process. The author compares it with voting on a classroom pet. Students mark their ballot by coloring in the picture of either a fish or a hermit crab. The book ends with the boy in the story going with his mom to vote.

Skills: Election Day

Grade Level: Kindergarten

Lesson

1. Greet students and show the cover and point to the words as you read the title. Explain that we are going to read about Election Day. Ask if any of them have heard their parent talk about going to vote.
2. Read the story slowly and stop to point out key things that explain the process.
3. Review the steps: collecting information, choosing, marking the ballot, and counting the votes.

Closure: Close by asking students if we vote on things at school. Make a list on the board. These may include voting on what kind of activities we will do on an inside recess day or voting for a kind of reward party. Dismiss students to check out.

Lesson 1

Election Day

By Lynn Peppas

Peppas, Lynn. *Election Day*. New York: Crabtree, 2011.

Summary: This book takes the reader through the election process and even explains the history of Election Day and why Tuesday was chosen. The text includes a Do You Know fact insert with trivia kind of information.

Skills: Election Day

Grade Level: First Grade

Materials: Poster paper
Marker

Instructions: Place the poster paper on a stand or easy-to-use easel.

Lesson

1. Most first graders have heard about the election from family members. Some will even give a person that they would vote for if they could go to the polls. Give students time to talk about the subject before showing the title and front cover of the book.
2. Select parts of the book to read and on which to focus. Each class may be different, so prepare by reading and marking pages that are better to read and talk about.
3. After the reading, review by asking the students to recall key facts. Some questions to ask may be as follows:

   Why do we hold election in November?
   Why do we vote on our leaders?
   What is a polling station?

Closure: End the storytime by taking the Election Day Quiz at the back of the book. Make sure to use only the questions that you covered in the reading if you chose to read only certain sections. Write the answers on the poster board. Dismiss students to check out.

Lesson 1

How Is a Government Elected?

By Susan Bright-Moore

Bright-Moore, Susan. *How Is a Government Elected?* New York: Crabtree, 2009.

Summary: A general overview of the election process from political parties to how to vote. The pictures and fact box inserts add to the appeal of the book.

Skills: Election Day
Collection of facts

Grade Level: Second Grade

Materials: Paper
Pencils

Instructions: Cut the paper into 4 by 6 inch size sheets.

Lesson

1. Share the front cover of the book and explain that the storytime will highlight a nonfiction or fact book about the election. Ask if anyone has heard about voting for a new leader from their parents. Give time for answers.
2. Read the book and share the pictures. Depending on the group of students, you might want to pick the important parts out or tell about some pages if it is too long for attention spans will vary.
3. Review the fact boxes and how they give us the extra facts that are interesting if we want to read more. Show the 4 by 6 inch cut papers and explain that each group will write out a fact they learned about voting. Be prepared to write words on the board that they might have trouble spelling.

Closure: Divide the students up with two or more to a group. Give each group a 4 by 6 inch size paper to record a fact. After they have recorded a fact, return to the group and share the facts that they remember. Dismiss students to check out.

VETERANS DAY LESSONS

Veterans Day is a lesser known holiday but is getting more and more popular in schools as young families with elementary students have dads and moms that serve in the military and participate in various hot spots around the world. Here are a few ideas that can be used either on a small scale or as a large school-wide event. Do not be afraid to ask the help of classroom teachers as they sometimes are looking for opportunities to tie into the curriculum.

1. Invite a family member of a student who has just returned from service to be a guest reader or speaker for the class. Before the event, take a large poster and write "Thank You for Your Service" across the front. Let each student sign the poster with markers and have it ready to give after the reading time or talk.

2. Students can make Christmas or other holiday cards to send overseas to service people. Sometimes a faculty member has a contact or a family member that is serving, and they can all be mailed to that person to give out to fellow service people.

3. Give the students time to draw and write thank you letters that can be taken or sent to a local Veterans Hospital. These are so welcomed by the patients. They enjoy reading letters from students and proudly display any and all art work that is sent to them.

4. Older students can make posters to hang around the school to honor veterans and help stress the importance of this holiday.

Lesson 2

Veterans Day

By Amanda Doering Tourville

Tourville, Amanda Doering. *Veterans Day*. Edna, MN: ABDO Publishing, 2008.

Summary: A general introduction to the holiday with the stress on how proud we are of those that have or are serving in the U.S. Military. It is complete with glossary and fun facts.

Skills: Veterans Day

Grade Level: Kindergarten

Lesson

1. Greet students and show the cover and point to the words as you read the title. Explain that we are going to talk about Veterans Day. Ask if any of them have any one in their family that is in the military service. Give time for comments. They will vary with each group, and sometimes even kindergarten students will have stories to share about their family.
2. Make sure to read the book ahead of time. Pick out parts of the book that need to be read and other pages that will just need to be talked about. Nonfiction books may be harder for this age-group, so keep it simple. Talking about some pages will make it easier for the students to grasp the important facts and hold their attention to the end.
3. Review any parts or words that might need extra clarification.

Closure: Close by standing and saying the pledge of allegiance or singing a patriotic song in honor of those that are serving. Dismiss students to check out.

Lesson 2

Veterans Day

By Robert Walker

Walker, Robert. *Veterans Day.* New York: Crabtree, 2010.

Summary: Pictures and easy-to-read text explain the holiday and how the day got started. The book covers symbols of Veterans Day and how we celebrate here in the United States.

Skills: Veterans Day

Grade Level: First Grade

Materials: Pull some easy nonfiction books about our country. These might include books about the American flag, Bald Eagle, Liberty Bell, and the military.

Instructions: Read the book ahead of time and mark pages that are most important.

Lesson

1. Most first graders have someone or have heard of someone that is serving in the military. Ask if someone can explain what the word "veteran" means. Give time for students to share. Check page 4 for the text that describes what a veteran is. Read that paragraph as you get started.
2. Read the parts that have been selected ahead of time. Each class may be different, so watch your group for interest and attention span.
3. After the reading, review by asking the students to recall key facts. Some questions to ask may be as follows:

   Who are veterans?
   Why do we have a special day to honor these soldiers?
   What are special events that we can do to honor these men and women?

Closure: Give time for students to look at the books that have been pulled ahead of time. They can pair up with a partner and share. Dismiss students to check out.

Lesson 2

Veterans Day

By Arlene Worsley

Worsley, Arlene. *Veterans Day.* New York: Weigl, 2011.

Summary: An easy-to-read introduction to the holiday and how it got started in the United States. Book will explain what other countries have a day where ceremonies take place. These countries call the day something else, but it is still a day to remember those who have served.

Skills: Veterans Day

Grade Level: Second Grade

Lesson

1. Share the front cover of the book and explain that the storytime will highlight a nonfiction or fact book about Veterans Day and how we celebrate. Ask students to share about family members or friends that serve in the military. Give time for answers. Explain that we have a special day set aside when we remember the service of veterans and say thank you.

2. Read the book and share the pictures. Pay close attention to words such as sacrifices, surrender, and patriot that might need extra time spent as explanation.

3. Review the fact boxes and how they give us extra facts that are interesting if we want to read more. Review the symbols at the back of the book and explain where they can be located.

Closure: Go over the Test Your Knowledge page and see if students can answer the questions. Dismiss students to check out.

THANKSGIVING LESSONS

Lesson 3

Run, Turkey, Run!

By Diane Mayr

Mayr, Diane. *Run, Turkey, Run!* New York: Walker & Company, 2007.

Summary: A turkey tries to avoid being cooked for Thanksgiving Day by hiding with various farm animals. The farmer and his family have to do without turkey because the turkey was successful in running away from the family. Repetitive phases throughout make for an excellent audience participating read aloud.

Skills: Role-play

Grade Level: Kindergarten

Materials: Chart paper or wipe-off board
  Maker
  Feather pattern
  Brown construction paper

Instructions: Make feathers, one for each student, from the brown construction paper. Write the repetitive words (Run, Turkey, Run!) on the chart paper or wipe-off board.

Lesson

1. Introduce the title and the author. Tell the students that they are going to participate in the story. Explain the word "participate." Example: Participate means you help with the story. Pass out the feathers and draw students' attention to the repetitive words on the paper or board. Describe to students that as the words "Run, Turkey, Run!" appear in the story, they need to wave their feather and say the works along with you. Practice so students will understand the concept. You might want to wave a feather too, so students will know when the repetitive words are coming in the story.

2. Read the story as the students participate. Ask the students if they enjoyed helping with the story. Invite students to share their favorite animal in the story.

Closure: Discuss the farmer's thanksgiving dinner. Invite students to share their favorite thanksgiving dishes other then turkey. Dismiss the students to check out.

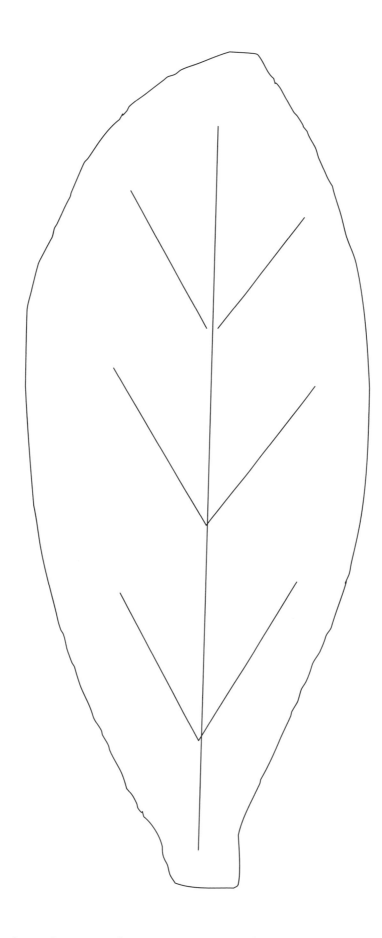

From *School Library Storytime: Just the Basics* written and illustrated by Brenda S. Copeland and Patricia A. Messner. Santa Barbara, CA: Libraries Unlimited. Copyright © 2013.

Lesson 3

Turkey Trouble

By Wendi Silvano

Silvano, Wendi. *Turkey Trouble*. Tarrytown, NY: Marshall Cavendish Children, 2009.

Summary: Turkey dresses as other animals in the barnyard to avoid being Thanksgiving dinner. As he doesn't have the body type for each of the animals, he becomes a pizza delivery guy, which saves his life.

Skills: Sorting descriptive words

Grade Level: First Grade

Materials: Old magazines
Card stock
Copy of descriptive words
Marker

Instructions: Find pictures of the animals in the story: horse, cow, pig, sheep, rooster, and turkey. Cut out and glue animal pictures onto 8-1/2 by 11 inch pieces of card stock. Using the marker, write the name of the animal on the card stock. Copy, cut apart, and glue the descriptive words onto 4 by 5-1/4 inch pieces of card stock. Laminate all pieces of card stock.

Lesson

1. Introduce the title and author. Tell the students there are five animals in the story and the author uses certain words for each animal, and those words helped the author describe the animals, so listen for those words, and we will play a sorting game after we read the story.
2. Read the story and share the pictures. Ask students if they heard some of the descriptive words.
3. Lay the picture of the animals in front of the class and pass out the descriptive words to students.
4. Explain to the students that they will need to match the words to the animals.

Closure: Encourage students to give other suggestions for descriptive words for the animals. Dismiss students to check out.

Too Short	Horsing Around
Holy Cow	Too Skinny
Quit Being a Ham	Too Clean
Baaa-d Idea	Too Brown
Cock-a-doodle-doo	Glove
Gobble, Gobble	Pizza

Lesson 3

Gus, the Pilgrim Turkey

By Teresa Bateman

Bateman, Teresa. *Gus, the Pilgrim Turkey.* Morton Grove, IL: Albert Whitman & Company, 2008.

Summary: Gus, the turkey, enjoys all the seasons and holidays leading up to Thanksgiving. After realizing people serve turkey on Thanksgiving, he travels south to Mexico and eventually hopping a ship heading further south. Gus ends up in the land of the penguins and they befriend Gus. The penguins called him a pilgrim since he traveled on a ship and he didn't feel safe just like the original pilgrims.

Skills: Answering questions about details

Grade Level: Second Grade

Materials: A copy of the penguin
               Marker
               Card stock

Instructions: Enlarge the penguin and copy onto card stock. Write questions on the penguins' bellies and laminate.

Lesson

1. Introduce the title and author. Show the cover of the book and allow time for students to share what they think the book will be about. Tell students to listen carefully to the story because there will be questions at the end of the reading.
2. Read the story and share the pictures.
3. Pass out the penguins with the questions on them to groups of two or three students. Allow time for students to collaborate with each other.
4. Call on groups of students to answer the questions.

Closure: Dismiss students to check out.

1. How do we know Gus is a young turkey?

2. Describe Gus's feelings at the beginning of the story.

3. Describe Gus's feelings at the middle of the story.

4. Describe Gus's feelings at the end of the story.

5. What did Gus pack in his backpack?

6. What were Gus's drumsticks?

7. How did Gus compare his situation to the pilgrims'?

8. Do you think Gus will enjoy penguin food?

9. Describe your favorite part of the story.

10. Describe the funniest page.

11. What did Gus wear to look like a penguin?

Lesson 4

What Is Thanksgiving?

By Elaine Landau

Landau, Elaine. *What Is Thanksgiving?* Berkeley Heights, NJ: Enslow Elementary, 2012.

Summary: A beginning nonfiction book about the origin of Thanksgiving. Starts with why the pilgrims celebrated Thanksgiving and ends with how we celebrate today. Complete with the table of contents, words to know, and index.

Skills: Introduction to a nonfiction book

Grade Level: Kindergarten

Materials: A fiction book about Thanksgiving that maybe you read last week

Lesson

1. Show the fiction book and ask the students if the book is a pretend book or a book that is about something real. Allow time for students to respond. Tell the students that when a book is a pretend story, it is called a fiction book.
2. Show the book *What Is Thanksgiving?* Have students look at the cover and ask if this book is a pretend story or a story about something that is real. Students should say that this book is about something real. Tell students that books that are about something real are called nonfiction.
3. Ask students: "What do you know about Thanksgiving?" Allow time for students to respond.
4. Read the story and share the pictures.
5. Compare the pictures in the fiction book with the book that was just read.
6. Talk about the information in the book and compare with what students already knew and what they know now about Thanksgiving.

Closure: Use the idea in the back of the book and make a poster or large card for a special person that the class would like to thank. Examples might be cooks, custodians, or other school staff. Dismiss students to check out.

Lesson 4

The Thanksgiving Bowl

By Virginia Kroll

Kroll, Virginia. *The Thanksgiving Bowl.* Gretna, LA: Pelican Publishing Company, 2007.

Summary: On Thanksgiving, at Grandma Grace's house, everyone writes things for which they are thankful on a piece of paper and places that paper in a yellow plastic bowl. This particular Thanksgiving, as the weather was warm, they celebrated outside. After Thanksgiving, the yellow bowl is left outside, and it rolls from place to place and ends up back at Grandma Grace's house by the next Thanksgiving Day.

Skills: Sequencing
  The months of the year

Grade Level: First Grade

Materials: Yellow plastic bowl
  Index cards or card stock
  A copy of the sequencing statements and months of the year

Instructions: Enlarge, copy, cut apart, and glue the statements and months of the year onto card stock or index cards. Glue the statement on one side and the month on the other and laminate. Place the cards in the yellow bowl to be used after reading the story.

Lesson

1. Introduce the title and author. Ask the students if they know the months of the year. Allow time for students to share. Tell the students that the months of the year will be mentioned as the story is read.
2. Read the story and share the pictures. Ask the students: Did you hear the months of the year? Do you remember what happened to the bowl during each month? Allow time for students to respond.
3. Show the yellow bowl and ask the students to tell you the purpose of the yellow bowl in the story. Talk about similar ways by which we can share what we are thankful for. For example, before eating Thanksgiving dinner, everyone says one thing that they are thankful for.

Closure: Allow time for students to sequence the events in the story using the cards that you prepared ahead of time. Students can try and put the statements in order or just the months. Dismiss students to check out.

The field mouse uses it for shelter.	December
A hat for the snowman	January
Beavers used it for a sled.	February
Geese lay eggs in the bowl.	March
Shaylyn hunted for fossils.	April
Alexandra planted flowers in the bowl.	May
Tori put tadpoles in the bowl.	June
Alyssa used the bowl to float her doll in the pool.	July
Christopher used it in the sandbox.	August
Tyler used it for a stepstool to fill the birdfeeder.	September
Raccoons played inside the bowl.	October
Back in Grandma Grace's yard.	November

 From *School Library Storytime: Just the Basics* written and illustrated by Brenda S. Copeland and Patricia A. Messner. Santa Barbara, CA: Libraries Unlimited. Copyright © 2013.

Lesson 4

Thanksgiving Rules

By Laurie Friedman

Friedman, Laurie. *Thanksgiving Rules.* New York: Carolrhoda Books, 2009.

Summary: Percy Isaac Gifford provides helpful rules for Thanksgiving. The illustrations are detailed with an abundance of graphics to keep readers pouring over the pages. Extra words that are written in a child's handwriting add information to the text.

Skills: Sequencing

Grade Level: Second Grade

Materials: Notebook paper
           Black marker
           Black construction paper

Instructions: Write the rules from the story on the notebook paper. One rule per sheet of paper. Glue the papers on black construction paper and laminate.

Lesson

1. Introduce the title and author. Tell the students that they are going to do a sequencing activity after reading this story, so they need to listen carefully.
2. Read the story and share the pictures, be sure to read all the extra words on the pages. If you forget to read them, the students will remind you.
3. Ask students to verbally tell you some of the rules from the story.
4. Mix the rules on the notebook pages up that you have prepared a head of time and have students try and put them in the order they appeared in the story.

Closure: Dismiss students to check out books.

RESOURCES

Authors

Calmenson, Stephanie. *Birthday at the Panda Palace*. New York: Harper-Collins, 2007.

Calmenson, Stephanie. *Jazzmatazz*. New York: HarperCollins, Children's Books, 2008.

Ehlert, Lois. *Rrralph*. New York: Beach Lane Books, 2011.

Henkes, Kevin. *Little White Rabbit*. New York: Greenwillow Books, 2011.

Henkes, Kevin. *My Garden*. New York: Greenwillow Books, 2010.

Martin, Bill. *Ten Little Caterpillars*. New York: Beach Lane Books, 2011.

Election Day

Harris, Nancy. *What Are Elections?* Chicago, IL: Heinemann Library, 2008.

Wells, Rosemary. *Otto Runs for President*. New York: Scholastic Press, 2008.

Veterans Day

Nelson, Robin. *Veterans Day*. Minneapolis: Lerner Publications, 2005.

Raven, Margot Theis. *America's White Table*. Ann Arbor, MI: Sleeping Bear Press, 2005.

Thanksgiving

Bildner, Phil. *Turkey Bowl*. New York: Simon & Schuster Books for Young Readers, 2008.

Bridwell, Norman. *Clifford's Thanksgiving Visit*. New York: Scholastic, 2010.

Gunderson, Jessica. *Life on the Mayflower*. Mankato, MN: Picture Window Books, 2011.

Lasky, Kathryn. *Two Bad Pilgrims*. New York: Viking, 2009.

Peppas, Lynn. *Thanksgiving*. New York: Crabtree, 2009.

Scieszka, Jon. *Trucksgiving*. New York: Simon Spotlight, 2010.

Stone, Tanya Lee. *T Is for Turkey: A True Thanksgiving Story*. New York: Price Stern Sloan, 2009.

Trueit, Trudi Strain. *Thanksgiving*. New York: Marshall Cavendish Benchmark, 2011.

1	2	3	4	5	6	7
8	9				13	14
15	16				20	21
22	23	24	25	26	27	28
29	30	31				

CHAPTER 4

DECEMBER

December is a busy and short month in the school calendar. Most schools' schedules include only two or three weeks of school for December, but we have included four lessons per grade level, so you probably won't use all the lessons. We concentrated on three holidays: Christmas, Hanukkah, and Kwanzaa. Another idea would be to celebrate Jan Brett's birthday by using some of her wonderful books during this month.

CHRISTMAS LESSONS

Lesson 1

Christmas Kitten, Home at Last

By Robin Pulver

Pulver, Robin. *Christmas Kitten, Home at Last.* Chicago: Albert Whitman & Company, 2010.

Summary: Cookie is a kitten without a home, and Santa wants to keep her. One big problem is that Santa is allergic to cats. Santa and Mrs. Claus have to find her a home. When they find a lost note that reads, "Please could I have a kitten for Christmas?," the problem is solved.

Skills: Sequencing

Grade Level: Kindergarten

Materials: Black, red, green, yellow, and blue construction paper

Instructions: Using the Christmas tree light pattern, make six lights. Label each light with one of these phrases: Cookie found, Santa sneezes, eggnog spilt, paw prints, ride in sleigh, welcome home. Where possible, place something that will help the students to read the phrases. For example, draw paw prints with the words or glue a tissue for the sneeze.

Lesson

1. Greet students and move with them to the story center. Show the cover and point to the words as you read the title. Ask students if they can predict the kind of book that will be read today. Responses will vary. This is a good time to explain how students can find a holiday book. If yours are labeled with a spine sticker, then remind them. Sometimes libraries set up a special section for the books they wish to highlight that month. If that is the case, remind them that the holiday books have been pulled and placed on a special shelf.
2. Read the story slowly and stop to talk about the kitten and what she is doing at that point.
3. After the reading, share the Christmas lights reading each phrase. Make sure to mix them up so that they do not get read in order. Point out that these were in the story and the task is to line them up as they appear in the book.
4. Call on individuals to come and pick out the correct one. Line them up on the floor for all to see.

Closure: Dismiss students to check out. Before the students return to class, review the story and cards.

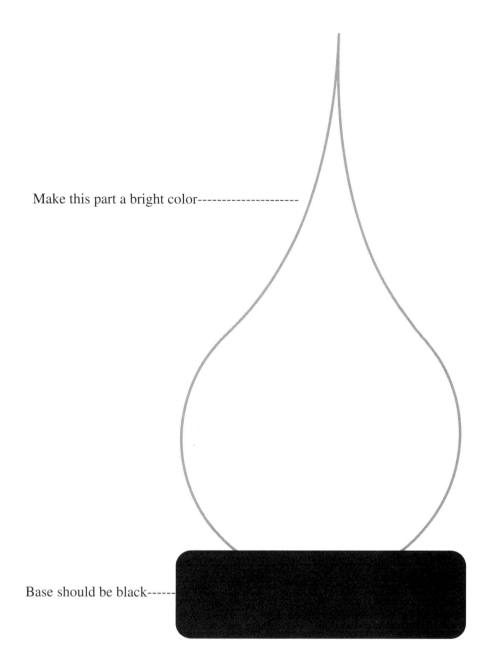

Make this part a bright color--------------------

Base should be black------

Lesson 1

Elmer's Christmas

By David McKee

McKee, David. *Elmer's Christmas*. Minneapolis: Lerner Publishing Company, 2010.

Summary: Elmer, the elephant, helps keep the younger elephants occupied while the older elephants wrap presents. The presents are picked up by Papa Red for those who need them the most. The younger elephants pick out and decorate a tree.

Skills: Joy of gift giving

Grade Level: First Grade

Materials: Copy of the package
　　　　　　Crayons
　　　　　　Pencils
　　　　　　Scissors
　　　　　　Christmas tree

Instructions: Copy the graphic of the package for each student.

Lesson

1. Introduce the title and author. Talk about gift giving. To whom do you give gifts? Do you ever give to people in need? How does our school give to those in need?
2. Read the story and share the pictures.
3. Discuss how the elephants gave to those in need.
4. Lead the students in a discussion of how they can give without buying gifts. Example: Help clean the house. Sit with the new student at lunchtime or play with that new student at recess.
5. Pass out the graphic of the package and have students color and write something they can do for someone else that would not cost any money.

Closure: Hang the packages on the tree in the library, or students may take them home to their tree. Dismiss students to check out.

Write an idea for a gift that doesn't cost any money.

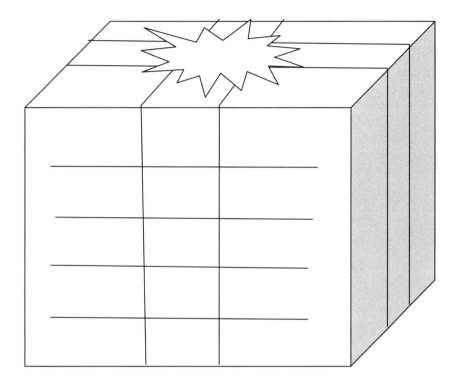

From *School Library Storytime: Just the Basics* written and illustrated by Brenda S. Copeland and Patricia A. Messner. Santa Barbara, CA: Libraries Unlimited. Copyright © 2013.

Lesson 1

Dewey's Christmas at the Library

By Vicki Myron and Bret Witter

Myron, Vicki and Bret Witter. *Dewey's Christmas at the Library*. New York: Little, Brown and Company, 2010.

Summary: Dewey, the library cat, enjoys the decorations in the library until the librarian takes the decorated tree and leaves Dewey alone for the weekend. On Monday morning, the librarian brings the tree back with a first place ribbon in a tree decorating contest.

Skills: Introduction to the Dewey Classification System

Grade Level: Second Grade

Materials: A copy of the Christmas tree graphic
                Crayons
                A copy of the call number for the cats' section
                One piece of card stock

Instructions: Copy the Christmas tree graphic for each student. Copy, enlarge, glue onto the card stock, and laminate the call number for the cats' section. Find a picture of Melvil Dewey either in a book or on the website http://www.encyclopedia.com/topic/Melvil_Dewey.aspx

Lesson

1. Introduce the title and author. Explain to the students the importance of the name Dewey. Show a picture of Melvil Dewey and tell the class that he created the number system for the nonfiction, and most libraries use this system.
2. Read the story and share the pictures. Show the call number for cats and tell the class that subjects have their own number in the Dewey Decimal System.
3. Pass out the Christmas tree graphic and give student guidance in decorating their tree with a favorite subject of theirs. If time allows and students know where their favorite subject is located, students can include the call number on their tree.

Closure: Allow time for students to decorate their tree and check out books.

Name_____.

My favorite subject in the library is_____.

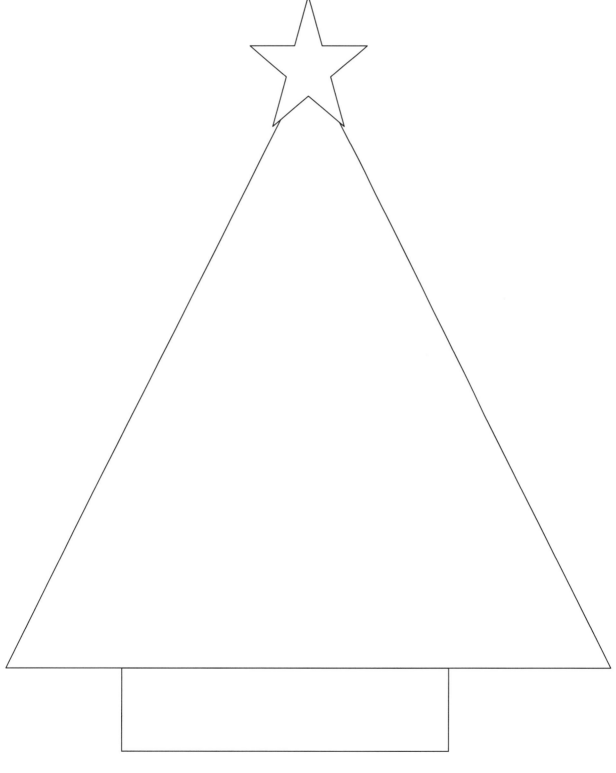

HANUKKAH LESSONS

Lesson 2

Hanukkah

By Trudi Strain Trueit

Trueit, Trudi Strain. *Hanukkah*. New York: Marshall Cavendish, 2011.

Summary: An introduction to the holiday with picture words and easy-to-follow text. Students can easily follow the eight pictures throughout the text and help with the reading. These include candles, chocolate coins, doughnuts, dreidel, gifts, latkes, and menorah.

Skills: Celebration of Hanukkah

Grade Level: Kindergarten

Materials: Drawing paper and crayons

Instructions: Prepare tables for drawing and coloring after the storytime. Write the picture words on the board so that the students can be reminded of what was discussed in the story.

Lesson

1. After reading the title and author on the title page, introduce the picture words that will be used in the text. These are located on the first two pages. Go over each one and give explanation were needed. Dreidel is a top and so on down through the list.

   An easy glossary is at the back. Read through the words and definition ahead of time so you are familiar with the item and how to pronounce the words.

2. Ask the students to look for these pictures and explain that they will be reading those as a group. Be sure to pause at each picture to let the group respond. Stop at words students are having problems remembering and reinforce and explain again what each of them means. The latkes might be hard to remember so you might have to explain they are similar to a pancake but made from potatoes after you use the word "latkes."
3. Review any part of the text that might need to be clarified.
4. End the time by stressing that some people celebrate Hanukkah instead of Christmas.

Closure: If time is available, give students drawing paper and let them draw some of the word pictures in the story. Dismiss students to check out.

Lesson 2

Runaway Dreidel!

By Leslea Newman

Newman, Leslea. *Runaway Dreidel!* New York: Henry Holt and Company, 2007.

Summary: A dreidel spins and runs away on an adventure, which teaches a little boy about celebrating Hanukkah.

Skills: Celebrating Hanukkah

Grade Level: First Grade

Materials: Pull some easy nonfiction books about Hanukkah. These should include ones with pictures of a menorah, dreidel, and candles.

Instructions: Look at the nonfiction books ahead of time and mark pages of items used in the celebration of Hanukkah.

Lesson

1. Most first graders have heard of Hanukkah, or they may call it the Festival of Lights. Remind the students that this story is about that celebration. Ask the students to listen for things that they do at the end of the story to celebrate Hanukkah.
2. Read and share the story to the class. Stop and point things out that might need more clarification.
3. Using the books that have been pulled ahead of time, share the pictures and talk about this holiday: How does it compare with Christmas? Do they give gifts? Do they get together as a family? Lead the discussion along these lines.

Closure: Give time for students to look at the books that have been pulled ahead of time. Dismiss students to check out.

Lesson 2

Jackie's Gift

By Sharon Robinson

Robinson, Sharon. *Jackie's Gift*. New York: Viking, 2010.

Summary: Jackie Robinson moves to Brooklyn and makes friends with a neighborhood kid named Steve. As Christmas begins to get nearer, Jackie asks his young friend if he has a tree. When Steve says no, Jackie decides to surprise the family with a tree. The only problem is that they are Jewish. A touching tale of how two families learn the lesson of unity.

Skills: Celebrating Hanukkah and Christmas

Grade Level: Second Grade

Materials: Poster paper
            Black marker

Lesson

1. Explain to the students that we are going to talk about unity today. Explain what the term means. Listen to the story for the ways that the characters show unity.
2. Read the book and share the pictures. Share with the students that the Jackie Robinson in the story eventually becomes a famous baseball player, and this is based on a true event that happened to him as a child. See Author's Notes at the end of the book.
3. Review with the students that Jewish families do not put up a Christmas tree. They light the menorah each night for eight nights, and kids would receive a gift on each night of Hanukkah. Watch the interest of the students and gage your discussion about this accordingly.

Closure: Talk about the word "unity." What does it mean? Make a list of things that second graders can do to practice unity at school. These might include making friends with that person in class that might be new or a special-needs student. Dismiss students to check out.

KWANZAA LESSONS

Lesson 3

Santa's Kwanzaa

By Garen Eileen Thomas

Thomas, Garen Eileen. *Santa's Kwanzaa*. New York: Jump at the Sun/ Hyperion Books for Children, 2004.

Summary: After Santa delivers presents to boys and girls, he comes home to a surprise. His wife and elves welcome him home with the beginning of Kwanzaa. They celebrate for a week and then Santa leaves to light up the sky with a message to all with his magic.

Skills: Celebrating Kwanzaa

Grade Level: Kindergarten

Materials: Wipe-off board
      Marker
      One black candle
      Three red candles
      Three green candles
      Individual candleholders or a large candleholder for seven candles

Instructions: Write the word "Kwanzaa" on the wipe-off board. You might want to research Kwanzaa on the Internet. Visit this website to gather facts before sharing with students: http://www.answers.com/topic/kwanzaa

Lesson

1. Draw students' attention to the word "Kwanzaa" that you have written on the board. Ask the students if they know anything about Kwanzaa. Allow time for students to respond. If you use this with kindergarten, students might not know much about this holiday. Tell students that Kwanzaa is a week-long celebration with a large feast and gift giving. A candle is lit each night. The black candle is for the people, red for their struggles, and the green for the future.
2. Introduce the title and author.
3. Read the story and share the pictures. Talk with students about Kwanzaa.

Closure: As students check out, show them where the nonfiction Kwanzaa books are located.

Lesson 3

Li'l Rabbit's Kwanzaa

By Donna L. Washington

Washington, Donna L. *Li'l Rabbit's Kwanzaa*. New York: Katherine Tegen Books, 2010.

Summary: Li'l Rabbit is too young to light the Kwanzaa candles and he can't remember the names of all the days of Kwanzaa. Granna Rabbit is sick and can't cook for the feast Karamu, so he ventures out to find something to help Granna Rabbit feel better. Li'l Rabbit meets many friends, and they help him bring the feast Karamu to the Rabbit Family.

Skills: Celebrating Kwanzaa
    Sequencing

Grade Level: First Grade

Materials: Candles and holders from Kindergarten Lesson
    Wipe-off board
    Marker
    Index cards or card stock
    Copies of the animal word cards and call numbers

Instructions: Display candles in holders for students to view during the lesson. Write Kwanzaa, Karamu, and Zawadi on the wipe-off board. Copy, enlarge, and glue the animal word cards and call numbers onto card stock or index cards. Laminate for longer use.

Lesson

1. Introduce the word "Kwanzaa" and ask students what they know about Kwanzaa. Allow time for students to respond.
2. Introduce the title and author. Tell the students that they are going to hear a story about Kwanzaa.
3. Read the story and share the pictures. Also share the last two pages of the book. These two pages have the seven days of Kwanzaa listed and definitions for Karamu and Zawadi.
4. Using the animal word cards, guide the students in sequencing the order Li'l Rabbit met the animals in the story.
5. Show students the call number for the book that was just read. Explain to the class that this is a fiction book but has true facts on the last two pages, and if they wanted more information about Kwanzaa, they would need to look in the nonfiction section under 394.2. Show students the call number for nonfiction Kwanzaa books and the location for the nonfiction Kwanzaa books.

Closure: Dismiss students to check out.

Oriole
Groundhog
Frog
Field Mouse
Squirrel

E WAS	394.2

Lesson 3

Kwanzaa

By Rissman, Rebecca

Rissman, Rebecca. *Kwanzaa.* Chicago: Heinemann Library, 2011.

Summary: This book introduces students to the holiday of Kwanzaa. Each page has photos of people celebrating. Included also are Kwanzaa symbols, a calendar, and picture glossary. The text uses African words and their meanings.

Skills: Celebrating Kwanzaa

Grade Level: Second Grade

Materials: Poster paper and marker
Paper cut into 3 by 5 inch strips (one per student)
Crayons, pencils, and glue

Instructions: Before the students arrive, list the seven important ideas that people think about during Kwanzaa. Write the African name beside each number and leave space for the English meaning. These will be filled in after the reading of the text. These include Umoja—Unity, Kujichagulia—Self-Determination, Ujima—Collective Work & Responsibility, Ujamaa—Cooperative Economics, Nia—Purpose, Kuumba—Creativity, and Imani—Faith.

Lesson

1. Explain that today the class will look at another holiday that is celebrated in December.

   It is Kwanzaa. It honors African history. It has some different ideas and celebrations. We need to pay close attention to how this holiday is different.

2. Read the title and share the front cover.
3. This book is short but has wonderful pictures that help explain the text. Stop after reading each section and talk about the pictures. Ask questions that will draw out discussion. Example: What are the children doing in this picture? Does it remind you of something you do in your home during the holidays? How is this holiday different from your holiday celebration?
4. Bring out the poster board and review the seven ideas that are important to this holiday. Write the English meaning next to the African word on the chart. Use the pictures in the book to remind students of what they stand for. Review some of the things they do during this time to celebrate. For example, play music, light candles, and eat together.

Closure: Give out small pieces of paper, crayons, and pencils. Let students draw pictures to decorate the poster. Talk about some things that might be good to help explain Kwanzaa and the seven important ideas. Students could draw the candleholder with the candles, calendar with the date of Kwanzaa, or the meaning of the African words. Allow time to glue them onto the poster around edges. If time is short, then they could be glued on by library staff, and poster can be displayed in a visible spot in the library. Dismiss students to check out.

DECEMBER LESSONS

Lesson 4

It's Christmas, David!

By David Shannon

Shannon, David. *It's Christmas, David!* New York: Blue Sky Press, 2010.

Summary: David tries to be good since Christmas is coming. Follow him through some antics that will surely keep his name on the naughty list. Simple text and pictures make this a favorite both to young readers and older ones alike.

Skills: Correct behavior

Grade Level: Kindergarten

Materials: Poster paper and marker

Instructions: Make a T chart on the poster paper and label one side with the word "naughty" and the other "nice."

Lesson

1. Greet students and move with them to the story center. Show the cover and point to the words as you read the title. Ask students what kind of book will we be reading today? Kindergarteners will recognize "David."

2. Read the story slowly and stop to talk about what David is doing in each picture. The text is really short, but this makes for a wonderful opportunity for students to share. Ask questions such as: What is David doing in this picture? Is this naughty or is this nice?

   Have you done anything like this at your house?

3. After the reading, point to the poster and tell the students that we will make a list of things that David did that were naughty. Then ask students to decide what David might have done differently that would have turned the naughty behavior into a nice one. Responses will vary. Students might need to be prompted in the right direction.

Closure: Ask students for a "thumbs-up" if they have been good this year. Will Santa come to their house? Are their names on Santa's Naughty List? Perhaps give them some time to discuss how to maintain the nice behavior. Dismiss students to check out.

Lesson 4

Ricky's Christmas Tree

By Guido Van Genechten

Van Genechten, Guido. *Ricky's Christmas Tree*. New York: Clavis Publishing, 2011.

Summary: Ricky's dad and mom are very busy, so they forgot about getting a Christmas tree, until Ricky reminded them. Ricky takes his time selecting a tree and observing the outdoors. On the way home with the tree, Ricky's dad stops trying to hurry Ricky up and they enjoy a snowball fight and other fun snow activities.

Skills: Author
Title
Characters
Setting

Grade Level: First Grade

Materials: Copy of the tree pattern
Copy of the ornaments
Green chart paper
Markers
Two-sided tape

Instructions: Enlarge the tree pattern onto chart paper and laminate. Enlarge ornaments, color with markers, cut out, and laminate. Apply the two-sided tape to the ornaments. Hang the tree on an easel or board so that the whole class can view it.

Lesson

1. Introduce the title and author. Tell the class to listen for the characters and setting. If this is the first time that you have talked about characters and setting, explain the meaning of these terms.
2. Read the story and share the pictures.
3. Pass out the ornaments and guide students in decorating the tree.

Closure: Dismiss students to check out.

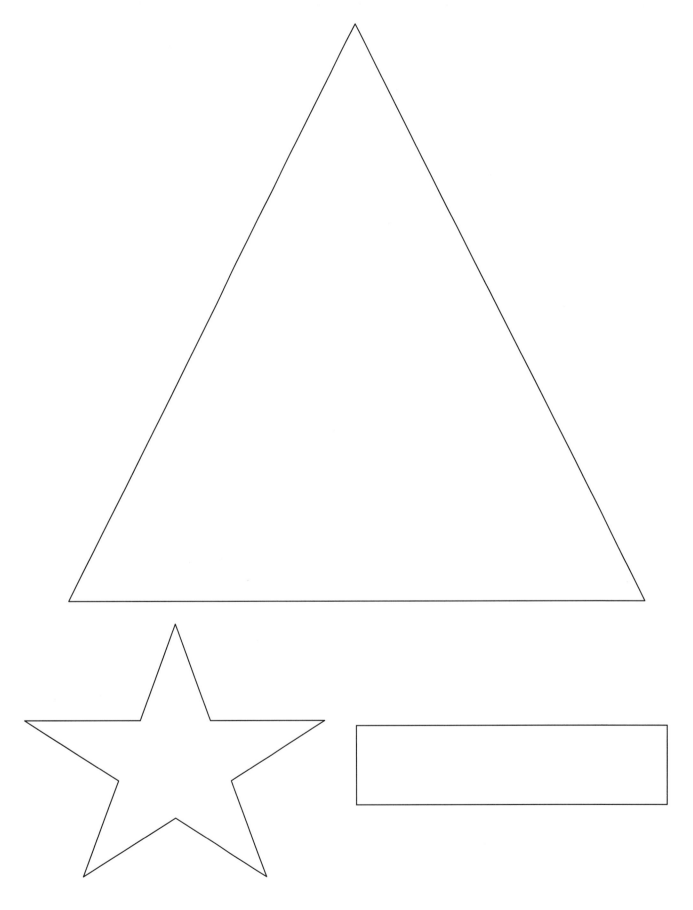

From *School Library Storytime: Just the Basics* written and illustrated by Brenda S. Copeland and Patricia A. Messner. Santa Barbara, CA: Libraries Unlimited. Copyright © 2013.

Winter

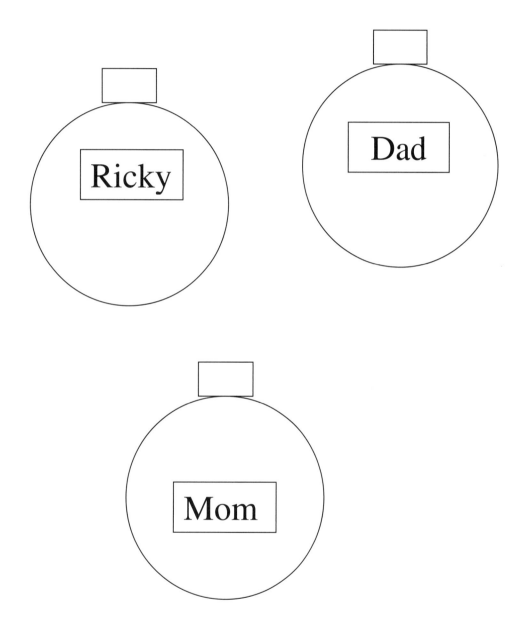

Ricky

Dad

Mom

Lesson 4

The Perfect Christmas

By Eileen Spinelli

Spinelli, Eileen. *The Perfect Christmas.* New York: Henry Holt and Company, 2011.

Summary: An unnamed girl in the book compares her family's Christmas with Abigail Archer's family Christmas. The rhyming text and collage pictures complete this simple story and make it an excellent read for comparing and contrasting.

Skills: Comparing and contrasting

Grade Level: Second Grade

Materials: A copy of the comparing and contrasting sheet
          Chart paper or wipe-off board
          Black marker

Instructions: Enlarge the comparing and contrasting sheet onto chart paper or a wipe-off board.

Lesson

1. Introduce the title and author. Tell the class that there will be two different families in the story and they celebrate Christmas in different ways. Listen and try to remember those differences.
2. Read the story and share the pictures.
3. Using the enlarged sheet, guide students in the completion.
4. Ask students to share which Christmas celebration is most like their celebration at home or their favorite.

Closure: Dismiss students to check out.

Compare and Contrast

Abigail Archer's Family	Little Girl's Family

From *School Library Storytime: Just the Basics* written and illustrated by Brenda S. Copeland and Patricia A. Messner. Santa Barbara, CA: Libraries Unlimited. Copyright © 2013.

RESOURCES

Christmas

Brett, Jan. *Home for Christmas.* New York: G. P. Putnam's Sons, 2011.

Bruel, Nick. *A Bad Kitty Christmas.* New York: Roaring Brook Press, 2011.

Buzzeo, Toni. *Lighthouse Christmas.* New York: Dial Books for Young Readers, 2011.

Cole, Brock. *The Money We'll Save.* New York: Margaret Ferguson Books, 2011.

Conover, Chris. *The Christmas Bears.* New York: Farrar Straus Giroux, 2008.

Dewdney, Anna. *Llama, Llama Holiday Drama.* New York: Viking, 2010.

Dunrea, Olivier. *Merry Christmas, Ollie!* Boston: Houghton Mifflin, 2008.

Grongan, John. *A Very Marley Christmas.* New York: HarperCollins, 2008.

Isadora, Rachel. *12 Days of Christmas.* New York: G. P. Putnam's Sons, 2010.

Lester, Helen. *Tacky's Christmas.* Boston: Houghton Mifflin, 2010.

Ransom, Candice F. *The Twelve Days of Christmas in Washington D.C.* New York: Sterling, 2010.

Trueit, Trudi Strain. *Christmas.* New York: Marshall Cavendish Benchmark, 2011.

Hanukkah

Baum, Maxie. *I have a Little Dreidel.* New York: Scholastic, 2006.

Heiligman, Deborah. *Celebrate Hanukkah.* Washington, DC: National Geographic, 2006.

Kroll, Steven. *The Hanukkah Mice.* New York: Marshall Cavendish, 2008.

Kropf, Latifa Berry. *It's Hanukkah Time!* Minneapolis: Kar-Ben Publishers, 2004.

Manushkin, Fran. *Latkes and Applesauce.* New York: Scholastic, 2007.

Martin, David. *Hanukkah Lights.* Somerville, MA: Candlewick Press, 2009.

Ofanansky, Allison. *Harvest of Light.* Minneapolis: Kar-Ben Publisher, 2008.

Penn, Audrey. *The Miracle Jar: A Hanukkah Story.* Terre Haute, IN: Tanglewood Press, 2008.

Kwanzaa

Aloian, Molly. *Kwanzaa.* New York: Crabtree Publishing, 2009.

It's Beginning to Look a Lot Like Kwanzaa! New York: Jump at the Sun/ Hyperion Books for Children, 2004.

Katz, Karen. *My First Kwanzaa.* New York: H. Holt, 2003.

			1	2	3	4
5	6				10	11
12	13				17	18
19	20	21	22	23	24	25
26	27	28	29	30	31	

CHAPTER 5

JANUARY

January is a long month with few holidays, so we have included some award-winning titles. For example, books that have won the Coretta Scott King and Caldecott awards. We have also created lessons for winter, the Chinese New Year, and Martin Luther King Jr. Day. Celebrating birthdays this month are Ian Feiffer, January 26 and Rosemary Wells, January 29.

SNOW LESSONS

Lesson 1

Kitten's Winter

By Eugenie Fernandes

Fernandes, Eugenie. *Kitten's Winter.* Toronto: Kids Can Press, 2011.

Summary: A kitten does not hibernate, but many other animals do. Simple text and collage illustrations show how many animals spend the winter.

Skills: Hibernating versus nonhibernating animals

Grade Level: Kindergarten

Materials: Copy of the sorting worksheet
Copy of the animal words
Chart paper
Card stock or index cards
Two-sided tape

Instructions: Copy the sorting worksheet onto the chart paper and laminate. Enlarge the animal words, glue onto the card stock or index cards, and laminate. Apply the two-sided tape to the animal word cards. Hang the chart paper so that the class can view.

Lesson

1. Introduce the title and author. Ask the students: Do you know what the word "hibernation" means? Allow time for students to share. If students have a hard time responding, help them out by explaining the meaning of hibernation.
2. Tell the students that some animals hibernate and other animals do not. Listen to the words and watch the pictures for hibernating and nonhibernating animals. Draw the students' attention to the chart paper and explain that we will complete this sheet together after the story.
3. Read the story and share the pictures.
4. Pass out the animal word cards and allow time for students to place the words on the correct side of the sheet. You might want to show the pictures as students place the cards on the sheet, especially if students are having a problem remembering.

Closure: Dismiss students to check out.

Turtle	Beaver
Bear	Chipmunk
Kitten	Fox
Raccoon	Woodpecker
Rabbit	Mouse
Otter	Squirrel

Hibernating Animals	Non-Hibernating Animals

Lesson 1

Snow Day!

By Lester L. Laminack

Laminack, Lester L. *Snow Day!* Atlanta: Peachtree, 2009.

Summary: When the news reports that a big snow is on the way, excitement run high in anticipation of all the fun that will be enjoyed with the closing of school the next day. Plans are made that include sledding, snow fort, and sleeping late the next morning. The house awakens to the sound of children running outside only to be surprised that they are not headed to go sledding or to make a snow fort, but they are going to have to go to school. The anticipated snow turns out to be only a few flurries. The end of the story is a twist, and the reader finds that it was the teacher who wanted the snow day the most. The surprise ending and illustrations are priceless.

Skills: Celebration of winter

Grade Level: First Grade

Materials: White copy paper
            Scissors

Instructions: Cut the copy paper into 4-inch blocks. Cut out a sample snowflake using one of the 4-inch blocks.

Lesson

1. Show the front of the book and ask a student to read the title.
2. Give students time to predict what might happen in the book. Ask them to explain their prediction.
3. Read the story and share the pictures. Stop on different pages and ask questions. Example: Are the characters in the story happy or sad? What clues tell you that they are happy? Why do the kids think they will have a snow day? What snow day activities are the kids planning if school is cancelled? What items will they need to carry out their plans? Example: Will they need their sleds? Who was disappointed the most at the end of the story? Were you surprised? Were you ever disappointed when plans changed at your house? Example: Your friend is planning on a sleepover for Friday night and that friend gets sick and the sleepover is cancelled. What did you do instead? Did the illustrator match up the drawings to the text?
4. Build up to the climax at the end. The students are surprised that the teacher is the one writing the story and is the one that needs a snow day. The students expect that they will have a big

snow at the end of the book. Some classes might need help with figuring out the ending. Give time at the end for comments and explanation.

5. This book lends itself to discussion about story endings and how the author can twist things so the reader is surprised.

Closure: The class should move to tables or an area for the cutting out of snowflakes. Share the sample that was cut before class. Fold and model another one for the class. Pass out paper and a pair of scissors. Collect and use the completed snowflakes to decorate the library. Dismiss students to check out.

Lesson 1

Utterly Otterly Night

By Mary Casanova

Casanova, Mary. *Utterly Otterly Night*. New York: Simon & Schuster Books for Young Readers, 2011.

Summary: The Otter family enjoys the snowy night until wolves appear. Little Otter is the first to see the wolves and he tries to warn his family, but he has to take drastic measures to alert the family. Many rhyming adjectives makes this book a fun read aloud.

Skills: Main characters
Supporting characters
Setting
Problem
Solution

Grade Level: Second Grade

Materials: Copy of the story elements sheet
Water base marker
Easel, wipe-off board, bulletin board

Instructions: Enlarge the story elements sheet and laminate. Hang the sheet on an easel, wipe-off board, or bulletin board so that students can access.

Lesson

1. Introduce the title and author. Tell students that they need to listen to the story and try to remember the characters, setting, problem, and solution.
2. Talk to the students about the main character and supporting characters.
3. Read the story and share the pictures.
4. Guide students in completing the story elements sheet. Students should take turns writing the story elements on the sheet. Enlist the class to help with spelling, and students might use the book to look up how to spell some of the characters. The supporting characters will be written on the points of the star.

Closure: Dismiss students to check out books.

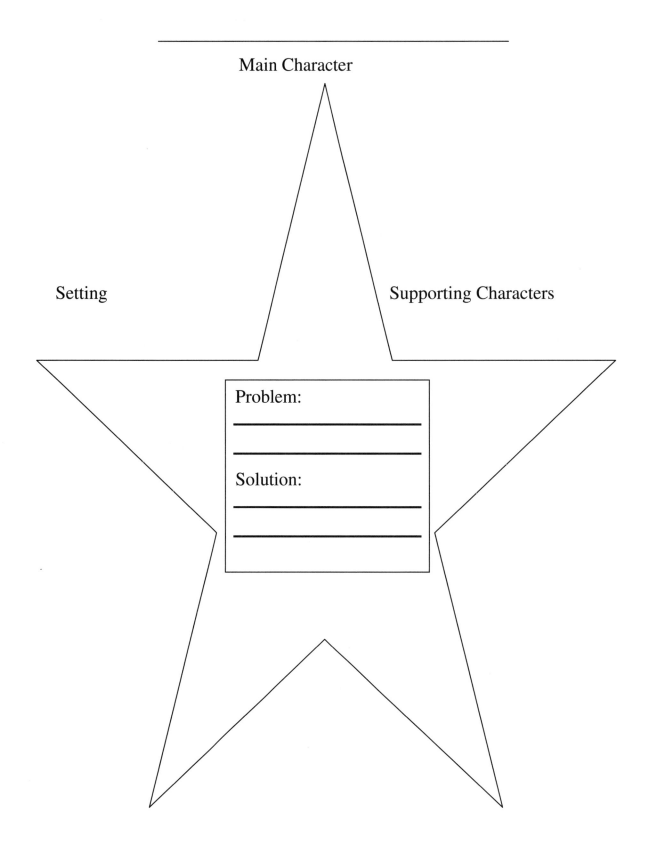

Main Character

Setting

Supporting Characters

Problem:

_____

_____

Solution:

_____

_____

MARTIN LUTHER KING JR. DAY LESSONS

Lesson 2

Martin Luther King Jr. Day

By Robin Nelson

Nelson, Robin. *Martin Luther King Jr. Day*. Minneapolis: Lerner, 2003.

Summary: This book with easy-to-follow text is a good introduction to Martin Luther King Jr. Day and how this holiday honors his name. The book contains a picture of a January calendar with the holiday marked, which makes a good visual for younger students. Photos add to the appeal of the book.

Skills: Celebration of Martin Luther King Jr. Day

Grade Level: Kindergarten

Materials: Construction paper, glue, and scissors
        Piece of yard about 36 inches long
        Copy of the timeline sheet attached to this lesson
        Poster board or small bulletin board

Instructions: Cut the boxes apart on the timeline sheet and mount on construction paper for longer wear. If these are being used for several classes, then laminate.

Lesson

1. Greet students and ask: What holiday is celebrated in January? Give time for the class to share. If students do not respond with the answer, then show the front of the book and read the title.
2. Explain that today's read aloud is a fact book with lots of interesting information about this holiday.
3. Read the book stopping to talk about the pages and events as you go along. Example: The calendar page makes a good opportunity to show what the day is. Point out today's date on the calendar and then the holiday. If school is closed for this holiday in your school district, then explain that this is one way we celebrate.
4. After reading, share the cards and go over what each one says. This is a good way to review the events in the life of Martin Luther King.

Closure: Create a timeline like the one found on pages 18 and 19 in the text. Explain that a timeline helps us see the events of a person's life better. If possible, staple it to a small board or piece of cardboard for a better visual picture for the students and use the piece of yarn to connect the events. Dismiss students to check out.

January 15, 1929 **Martin was born**	**1963** **"I Have a Dream"** **Speech**
1964 **Nobel Peace Prize**	**1968** **Shot**
1983 **Signed in law** **Holiday is official**	**1986** **First celebration** **of this holiday**

Lesson 2

My Uncle Martin's Big Heart

By Angela Farris Watkins

Watkins, Angela Farris. *My Uncle Martin's Big Heart.* New York: Abrams Books for Young Readers, 2010.

Summary: The story is told from the pen of the niece of Martin Luther King Jr. Angela introduces the reader to the special memories of her uncle and includes family events that give us a different view of this well-known figure. The book focuses on the positive love that he shared.

Skills: Celebration of Martin Luther King Jr. Day

Grade Level: First Grade

Materials: Poster paper and marker

Instructions: Place the poster paper on a stand or easy-to-use easel.

Lesson

1. Most first graders have heard about Martin Luther King Jr. Most classroom teachers would have introduced the topic to their students. Hold up the book and explain that Martin Luther King's niece wrote this story about her uncle. Point out how the illustrator pictured the author and her uncle on the front.
2. Does anyone have a favorite uncle? What kind of things do you do with this uncle? Why do you like this uncle? Give time for students to share. This will vary with each class. Watch that one or two students do not do all the talking. Keep the sharing time moving so that many students have an opportunity to talk.
3. Ask the students to listen for the events that the author thought were special about her uncle.
4. Read the story and share the pictures.

Closure: End the storytime by making a list of the special family moments that the author shared with her uncle. They might include sent telegrams, spent the night, made his family laugh, gave his niece hugs, and talked with his family. If time allows, go back to the sharing that the students did at the beginning of the storytime. Do any of those things remind them of what Martin Luther King did with his family? Dismiss students to check out.

Lesson 2

Riding to Washington

By Gwenyth Swain

Swain, Gwenyth. *Riding to Washington*. Chelsea, MI: Sleeping Bear Press, 2008.

Summary: A little white girl and her father travel on a bus to Washington, DC, to hear Martin Luther King's "I Have a Dream" speech. They travel with mostly black people from Indiana. The day is long, and when they stop at a restaurant, they are not served because the restaurant does not offer service to mixed racial crowds. They also ask the bus driver to stop for a restroom break, and the little girl talks the boy at the gas station into letting them use the restroom usually reserved for white guests only. They arrive hungry and tired but joyful that they are able to hear the famous speech.

Skills: Comprehension

Grade Level: Second Grade

Materials: Comprehension questions from the given lesson
　　　　　Bus pattern
　　　　　Blue construction paper
　　　　　Marker

Instructions: Copy the bus pattern onto the blue construction paper. Cut out and write the questions on the back of the buses. Laminate for longer life.

Lesson

1. Introduce the title and author. Tell the students that they will need to listen carefully because there are questions at the end of the story. Also inform the students that this book is about Martin Luther King's "I Have a Dream" speech. If students do not know anything about the speech, elaborate more.
2. Read the story and share the pictures.
3. Pass the questions written on the buses out to the class. Give a question to groups of two or three students and have them collaborate and be ready to answer the question.

Comprehension Questions

What do you think the bus riders said when they could not stop at the restaurant?

Has your mother or father ever said, "You are trouble with a capital T"?

How did the riders take their minds off their problems?

What do you do in the car when you can't stop for food?

What was your favorite part?

If you were in a similar situation as the little girl, how would you handle it?

What songs would you sing?

Closure: Dismiss students to check out.

From *School Library Storytime: Just the Basics* written and illustrated by Brenda S. Copeland and Patricia A. Messner. Santa Barbara, CA: Libraries Unlimited. Copyright © 2013.

CHINESE NEW YEAR LESSONS

Lesson 3

Chinese New Year

By Nancy Dickmann

Dickmann, Nancy. *Chinese New Year*. Chicago: Heinemann Library, 2011.

Summary: This is a simple introduction to the Chinese New Year with colorful pictures and easy-to-follow text. Included in the text is a look-and-see page of the animals that are used to celebrate this holiday. One animal represents each year.

Skills: Celebration of Chinese New Year

Grade Level: Kindergarten

Materials: Drawing paper and crayons
Poster paper and marker

Instructions: Before class starts, prepare a giant T on the large poster paper. Label one side of the T with the title Chinese New Year and the other with American New Year.

Lesson

1. Ask students to share what they do to celebrate the New Year. Give time for responses.
2. Show the front of the book and explain that today we are learning how the Chinese celebrate their new year. Point out that the Chinese New Year celebrations last for 15 days.
3. Read the book and share the pictures.
4. After reading the book, help the kids remember how the Chinese celebrate the New Year. Make a list on the Chinese side of the T chart. The list might include visiting family, eating food, wearing new clothes, giving gifts, watching fireworks, and hanging red banners.
5. After recording the Chinese celebration, ask the students for ways that people in the United States celebrate the new year. These will vary, and the students might need help. One way is to go down the Chinese list and ask, do we celebrate this, and if so, then discuss, compare, and note on the U.S. side of the T. If not, then ask them what we do. Some will be the same: visiting family, eating food, and watching fireworks.

Closure: Dismiss students to check out. If time is available, give students drawing paper and let them draw pictures of their family's celebration of the New Year.

Lesson 3

A New Year's Reunion

By Yu Li-Qiong

Li-Qiong, Yu. *A New Year's Reunion.* Somerville, MA: Candlewick Press, 2011.

Summary: Maomao's papa works far away and comes home only during the Chinese New Year. She celebrates with her parents and friends. Papa hides a fortune coin in a stick rice ball and Maomao finds the coin. She carries the coin everywhere until, after playing in the snow, she discovers the coin missing. Maomao looks for the coin but cannot find it until she goes to bed and it drops on the floor.

Skills: Celebrating Chinese New Year

Grade Level: First Grade

Materials: Wipe-off board or chart paper
　　　　　　 Marker

Instructions: Research the Chinese New Year before class time. Use this website or find another one. www.infoplease.com/spot/chinese-newyear1.html

Lesson

1. Introduce the title and author. Ask the class if they know anything about the Chinese New Year. Allow time for students to respond and share. Share facts that you research before students come to the library. Record the facts on the board or chart paper.
2. Read the story and share the pictures. Discuss the things that Maomao and her mom and dad did in the story. Record any that were not recorded earlier.

Closure: Dismiss students to check out.

Lesson 3

The Runaway Wok

By Ying Chang Compestine

Compestine, Ying Chang. *The Runaway Wok*. New York: Dutton Children's Books, 2011.

Summary: When Mama Zhang sends her son Ming to the market to trade a few eggs for some rice, Ming brings back an old rusty wok. Ming was told by an old man that it was a magic wok. When the wok arrives at Ming's house, it sings a song that tells the family to polish it up. After it is polished, it runs away to the rich man's house where it is filled with good food. The wok then runs away again to the poor family. This happens three more times where it brings back gifts and money and finally carries the rich family away to the mountains where they are not heard from again. Ming and his family share the good fortune with their neighbors. The wok helps the poor families celebrate the New Year.

Skills: Celebrating Chinese New Year

Grade Level: Second Grade

Lesson

1. Share the front cover and explain that today's story is about the celebration of Chinese New Year.
2. Read the book and share the pictures.
3. Review with the students the events of the story. Ask them the following questions that will move the discussion along more easily. How many times did the wok go to the rich man's house? What did the wok bring back each time? How did that help the poor families celebrate the New Year?

Closure: Ask students if they can make connections to other stories where there is a character that runs away. These might include the Gingerbread Man running away from the little old man and women, Goldilocks running away from the three bears, and the little pigs running away from the wolf. Once the class has pointed out these simple ones, they will make other connections that will surprise you. Dismiss students to check out.

AWARD-WINNING LESSONS

Lesson 4

A Ball for Daisy

By Chris Raschka

Raschka, Chris. *A Ball for Daisy*. New York: Wade Books, 2011.

Summary: A wordless picture book about how a dog loses his ball and makes a friend. This is the 2011 Caldecott Medal winner.

Skills: Award books—Caldecott

Grade Level: Kindergarten

Materials: Collection of Caldecott winners

Instructions: Pull some easier Caldecott winners from previous years. These might include *Owl Moon* by Jane Yoland, *A Sick Day for Amos McGee* by Philip C. Stead, and *Kitten's First Full Moon,* by Kevin Henkes.

Lesson

1. Greet students and explain that today we are going to look at a special book that has received an award. What does it mean to receive an award? Explain this if no one gives an answer. Show the front of the book and title.
2. Point out to the class that a group of people each year read and look at lots of picture books. After reviewing all the new books that were published for the year, they vote on the one that they think is best. This process is a very hard job. The award is called the Caldecott Award and the book is judged on just the pictures.
3. Since this is a wordless book, you will need to pick students to take turns picture talking the story. Move through the story. Do not rush. The students will enjoy getting to be chosen to talk. Ask that student to come to the front and help hold the book while they are talking. Some students might need a little help with the process of explaining the picture. Pick students that are sitting quietly.
4. If your library marks the Caldecott books with a special spine sticker, point this out and show where that is located on the book spine.
5. Pair up the students with a partner and have them go to the everybody (easy) section and see if they can find another Caldecott book that has a special sticker. Have the students raise their hand and stand beside the shelf when they have located one. If your library does not have stickers on the spines, then skip down to the closing activity instead.
6. Dismiss students to check out.

Closure: Have the students move back to the story circle. Show the few books that have been pulled ahead of time. Page through the stories and show the students that each book has different kinds of pictures. Some are colored and others are black-and-white drawings. If any of the books have a gold Caldecott seal on the front, point this out.

Lesson 4

My People

By Langston Hughes

Hughes, Langston. *My People.* New York: Ginee Seo Books, 2009.

Summary: A poem set to photographs depicting African Americans in many expressions. This book is a wonderful example of photographic illustrations.

Skills: Illustrations

Grade Level: First Grade

Materials: A copy of Jim Borgman's poster "How Are You Feeling Today?"
A copy of the Coretta Scott King Award poster

Instructions: Obtain a copy of the Coretta Scott King Award poster. Follett and Perma Bound will give these to you free of charge. Display for all students to view. You might want to pull a few other books that have won the award in years past.

Follett Library Resources
1340 Ridgeview Drive
McHenry, Illinois 60050–7048

Perma-Bound
617 E. Vandalia Road
Jacksonville, Illinois 62650

Purchase a copy of the poster "How Are You Feeling Today?" or if you have access to a projector and computer, pull the poster up on the website www.feelingsunlimited.com/poster.html. Display for all students to view.

Lesson

1. Draw students' attention to the Coretta Scott King Award poster. Show students the left-hand side of the poster. Tell the students about the illustrator part of the award. If students ask about the author side, just tell them that those are for older students to read.
2. Introduce the title and author. Explain to the students that this book is a poem with photographs as the illustrations. Show the students the poster "How Are You Feeling?" Tell the students that the photographs in this book are mostly facial expressions, and we will talk about the expressions and compare them with the poster.
3. Read the book and share the pictures.

Closure: Look back through the book and match the facial expressions to the poster. Dismiss students to check out.

Lesson 4

Dave the Potter: Artist, Post, Slave

By Laban Carrick Hill

Hill, Laban Carrick. *Dave the Potter: Artist, Poet, Slave.* New York: Little, Brown and Company, 2010.

Summary: A beautifully illustrated book documenting the skill of Dave the potter. Included are several photos of the actual pieces of pottery that have survived. Extra pages provide lines of poetry written by Dave and extra resources.

Skills: Biography
          Sequencing

Grade Level: Second Grade

Materials: Copy of the biography call number
               Copy of the sequencing sheet
               Card stock
               Coretta Scott King Award poster—see first-grade lesson

Instructions: Copy the call number and sequencing sheet onto card stock, cut out, and laminate.

Lesson

1. Introduce the title and author. Using the poster, tell students that this book is a Coretta Scott King Award-winning book. It is also a biography book; review the biography section and show the students the call number.
2. Read the story and share the pictures.
3. Talk about the process of making a clay pot. Show the authentic pictures of Dave's pottery.
4. Show the sequencing cards and allow time for students to put the cards in order.

Closure: Using the dates on the last few pages of the book, create another sequencing activity. Students may sequence the dates during checkout time. Dismiss students to check out.

B DAV	Scoops Dirt
Mixed Dirt & Water	Threw the clay
Kicked the potter's wheel	Pinched the top edge
Spins the potter's wheel	Rolled long ropes
Mounted ropes	Makes Glaze

RESOURCES

Caldecott Award

http://ala.org/alsc/awardsgrants/bookmedia/caldecottmedal/
caldecottmedal

Levine, Ellen. *Henry's Freedom Box.* New York: Scholastic, 2007.

Pinkney, Jerry. *The Lion & the Mouse.* New York: Little, Brown and Company, 2009.

Stead, Philip C. *A Sick Day for Amos McGee.* New York: Roaring Brook Press, 2010.

Swanson, Susan Marie. *The House in the Night.* Boston: Houghton Mifflin Company, 2008.

Chinese New Year

Chen, Yong. *A Gift.* Honesdale, PA: Boyds Mills Press, 2009.

Flanagan, Alice K. *Chinese New Year.* Minneapolis: Compass Point Books, 2004.

Gleason, Carrie. *Chinese New Year.* New York: Crabtree, 2009.

Katz, Karen. *My First Chinese New Year.* New York: Holt, 2004.

Coretta Scott King Award

Bryan, Ashley. *Let It Shine: Three Favorite Spirituals.* New York: Atheneum Books for Young Readers, 2007.

Giovanni, Nikki. *Rosa.* New York: Scholastic Inc., 2005.

Klingel, Cynthia. *Coretta Scott King.* Mankato, MN: The Child's World, 2010.

Weatherford, Carole Boston. *Moses: When Harriet Tubman Led Her People to Freedom.* New York: Jump at the Sun/Hyperion Books for Children, 2006.

Martin Luther King Jr Day

Evans, Shane W. *We March.* New York: Roaring Brook Press, 2012.

Farris, Christine King. *March On! The Day My Brother Martin Changed the World.* New York: Scholastic Press, 2008.

Kittinger, Jo S. *Rosa's Bus.* Honesdale, PA: Calkins Creek, 2010.

Miller, Reagan. *Martin Luther King, Jr. Day.* New York: Crabtree, 2009.

Mis, Melody S. *Meet Martin Luther King Jr.* New York: Powerkids Press, 2008.

Reynolds, Aaron. *Back of the Bus.* New York: Philomel Books, 2010.

Shelton, Paula Young. *Child of the Civil Rights Movement.* New York: Schwartz & Wade Books, 2010.

Winter

Butler, M. Christina and Tina Macnaughton. *Snow Friends.* Intercourse, PA: Good Books, 2005.

De Haas, Rick. *Peter and the Winter Sleepers.* New York: North-South Books, 2008.

Flanagan, Alice K. *Snow.* Mankato, MN: The Child's World, 2010.

Randall, Angel and Chris Schoebinger. *Snow Angels.* Stevens Point, WI: Worzalla Publishing Co., 2011.

Scieszka, Jon. *Snow Trucking!* New York: Aladdin, 2008.

Teitelbaum, Michael. *Baby Polar Bears' Snow-Day.* San Anaselmo, CA: Treasure Bay, 2009.

Thomas, Patricia. *Red Sled.* Honesdale, PA: Boyds Mills Press, 2008.

						1
2	3				7	8
9	10				14	15
16	17	18	19	20	21	22
23	24	25	26	27	28	

CHAPTER 6

FEBRUARY

February is full of holidays to highlight in any library program. 100th Day of School, Presidents' Day, Groundhog Day, and Valentine's Day are a few special days to celebrate. Black History and Dental Health are month-long themes that can be used. Mo Willems celebrates his birthday on February 11 along with Jane Yolen.

GROUNDHOG'S DAY LESSONS

Lesson 1

Punxsutawney Phyllis

By Susanna Leonard Hill

Hill, Susanna Leonard. *Punxsutawney Phyllis.* New York: Holiday House, 2005.

Summary: Phyllis sees all the signs of spring, and Uncle Phil decides to retire. Uncle Phil gives his job to Phyllis, which is to predict the weather. Phil Jr. and Pete are disappointed because a girl has never had the job.

Skills: Main character
Supporting characters

Grade Level: Kindergarten

Materials: Copy of the hat
Copy of the characters' names
Chart paper
Marker
Tape

Instructions: Enlarge the hat pattern onto chart paper and laminate. Also cut out the characters' names and laminate for longer life. Display the hat so all students can view.

Lesson

1. Introduce the title and author. Talk about the main character and supporting characters. Explain that the main character appears in the story the most and is very important. The supporting characters help the main character to make the story enjoyable. Tell the students to listen for the main and supporting characters as you read the story.
2. Read the story and share the pictures. Ask the students: Do you remember some of the characters? Read and show the characters' names that have been cut out and laminated.
3. Pass out the characters' names and have the students decide where on the hat that each one of them belongs.
4. Tape the names in the correct spots.

Closure: Dismiss students to check out.

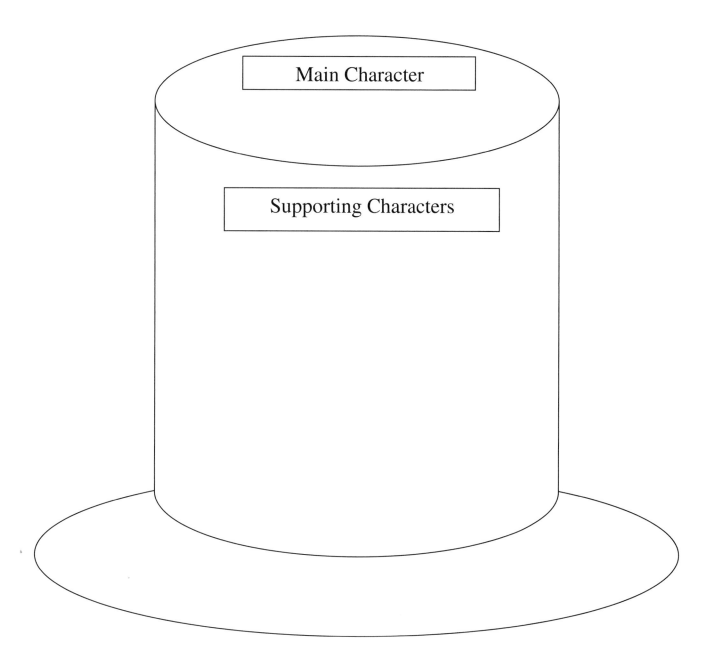

Main Character

Supporting Characters

Mother	Father	Aunt Patsy
Aunt Sassy	Uncle Phil	Phil Junior
Phyllis	Grandfather	Pete

Lesson 1

Groundhog Weather School

By Joan Holub

Holub, Joan. *Groundhog Weather School.* New York: Putnam's Sons, 2009.

Summary: Groundhog needs help all over the country to determine when spring will be, and so he sets up a school to teach young groundhogs how to forecast the weather. The book includes facts as part of the story so that young readers really can learn about this holiday in a fun way.

Skills: Groundhog Day

Grade Level: First Grade

Materials: Stickers for each student

Instructions: Read and study the text before reading. This is a cute story but does have a lot of extra material about Groundhog Day interwoven into the pictures and text. Some of the pages you will want to read and others you will want to talk about. For example, at the groundhog school, Prof. Groundhog explains how to make a burrow. This page of artwork showing the inside of a burrow is one you might want to just talk about. The page with the "Pledge of Hog-Allegiance" that the groundhogs take at the start of school might be one that you will want to read.

Lesson

1. Greet students and ask: What holiday is celebrated on February 2? Give time for the class to respond. Students will enjoy sharing because this is a much talked-about topic in the lower elementary grades. Let them explain what they already know about the topic before reading the book.
2. Share the front cover of the book and title. Read the book stopping to talk about the pages and events as you go along.
3. After reading, ask the students if groundhog school is like regular school. How is it different?

Closure: Just for fun, see if the students can answer the multiple-choice test that the groundhogs had to take. When they have finished answering the questions, tell the students that they could be groundhog helpers. Give each student a sticker as a reward for being good listeners. Dismiss students to check out.

Lesson 1

Brownie Groundhog and the February Fox

By Susan Blackaby

Blackaby, Susan. *Brownie Groundhog and the February Fox.* New York: Sterling, 2011.

Summary: Brownie Groundhog walks outside on February 2 and sees her shadow. She is carrying a snack and meets up with a fox. The fox wants to eat Brownie, but Brownie detours the fox by playing in the snow. Brownie shares her snack, which satisfies the fox. They go home promising to meet back tomorrow, and Brownie agrees to bring something yummy.

Skills: Compare and contrast

Grade Level: Second Grade

Materials: A version of *The Gingerbread Man*
          Chart paper
          Marker

Instructions: Draw a T chart on the chart paper. Write "Brownie's Behavior" on one side and "Fox's Behavior" on the other side. Display so all students can view. Read *The Gingerbread Man* before class starts so that you can summarize the story for the class.

Lesson

1. Show the students *The Gingerbread Man* and summarize the fox's behavior in the story. Write fox's behavior on the chart paper. Examples might be jump on my tail, jump on my back, jump on my head, and so on.
2. Introduce the title and author and tell the students that we are going to compare Brownie's behavior with the fox's behavior.
3. Read the story and share the pictures. Allow time for students to recall Brownie's behavior in the story. Record the behaviors on the chart. Examples might be too late for breakfast, too early for lunch, you haven't worked up an appetite, and so on.
4. Compare and contrast the behavior of both the animals in different stories.

Closure: Dismiss students to check out books.

Brownie's Behavior	Fox's Behavior
(Brownie Groundhog and the February Fox)	(The Gingerbread Man)
Too Late for Breakfast!	Jump on my back!

100TH DAY LESSONS

The 100th day of school is a much celebrated holiday in elementary schools. As classroom teachers look forward to this milestone, they plan activities that tie into math and other curricular areas. Many do community outreach by collecting soup cans for shelters or organizations that help needed families. Hats are created and parades are enjoyed as the school laughs and gets into the party mood. The library can tie into this school event by planning literacy connections that involves the whole school. Here are a few that seem to be favorites.

1. Counting books

As each class comes into the library during the week of the celebration, let the students create a book chain that will tell how many books have been checked out for that time period. Make it easier to count by tens by making the tenth chain a different color. Cut out strips of paper ahead of time and map out a place where the pasting can take place. As each student checks out books, let them add to the chain. Hang the chain in the library. Using school colors for the paper chain is a good way to promote school spirit and unity at the same time.

2. Counting minutes

As lessons are finished in the library each day, give students time for silent reading. Keep a count of the total time, in minutes, read all week. Keep a running total all week and ask a different class to help total the amounts each day. Post on a bulletin board for all to see. Give special treat to the class each day that pushes the day's total to 100 or more.

3. Reading books

On a large poster, print the words "100 books read at _____ Elementary School." Fill the space around it with the titles of books that have been read that week. The library staff might want to do the printing so that there is enough room for all 100 books.

Lesson 2

It's the 100th Day, Stinky Face!

By Lisa McCourt

McCourt, Lisa. *It's the 100th Day, Stinky Face!* New York: Scholastic, 2010.

Summary: Follow a little boy through the excitement of choosing what to bring into school for the 100th day. It has to be 100 of something. He keeps asking his mother if he can bring hard things that would be impossible to manage. Finally, he decides to bring his questions because he surely has asked 100 different ones.

Skills: 100th day

Grade Level: Kindergarten

Materials: Poster paper and marker
Cartload of returned library books

Lesson

1. Greet students and show the cover and point to the words as you read the title. Ask if any of them have heard of 100. How do we write this number? Write it out on the poster paper.
2. Read the story and ask if the some of the items the little boy asked to bring each time could have been brought to school. For example: Could the little boy bring 100 stars from the sky?

Closure: Close by letting the students count the number of books that have been returned to the library today. If this is the first class, then you might not have 100, but it will get the kids thinking about what makes up 100. Dismiss students to check out.

Lesson 2

Fancy Nancy: The 100th Day of School

By Jane O'Connor

O'Connor, Jane. *Fancy Nancy: The 100th Day of School.* New York: HarperCollins, 2009.

Summary: Fancy Nancy is having trouble finding something really special to bring in for the 100th day of school. She does not want it to be just ordinary but something imaginative.

Skills: 100th day

Grade Level: First Grade

Materials: Poster paper and marker

Instructions: Using the fancy word list at the back of the text, print out the fancy words that Fancy Nancy uses. Leave space beside them to write out the ordinary words.

Lesson

1. All first graders have heard of Fancy Nancy and her books go out all the time. Show the title and review where these books are located in the library. You might like to pull some extra ones ahead of time for students to look at if there is time at the end of the storytime.
2. Before reading, ask: What do you think Fancy Nancy should take to school to celebrate the 100th day? Give time for students to respond.
3. After the reading, review by asking the students to recall all of the things that Nancy did not pick to bring to school.

Closure: Show the poster with the fancy words written out. Ask for volunteers to explain what the fancy words mean. If no one remembers, then return to the text and read the page again. Write in the correct ordinary word beside the fancy word. Dismiss students to check out.

Lesson 2

Jake's 100th Day of School

By Lester L. Laminack

Laminack, Lester L. *Jake's 100th Day of School.* Atlanta, GA: Peacetree, 2006.

Summary: Jake is so excited to celebrate the 100th day of school. Only problem is, he runs to catch the bus but forgets his project. The principal saves the day and helps Jake out.

Skills: 100th day

Grade Level: Second Grade

Materials: Two pieces of poster paper and marker

Instructions: At the top of the poster board, write a message to the principal in bold black letters.

Example: "Thank you for all the 100 things you do for us every day" or "Thank you, Principal _____(name of the principal). We think you are special."

Lesson

1. Share the front cover of the book and explain that the story is about the 100th day of school. Ask what kind of projects they are working on in their classrooms. It might be helpful ahead of time to talk with the second-grade teachers so you get a feel of what is going on in the classroom. Talk about the excitement of collecting the items and how they plan to arrange them.
2. Read the book and share the pictures. Since the principal helped Jake out, talk about all the special things that the principal does at your school. Is the job of principal hard? Create a list on one piece of the poster paper of things as students share.

Closure: During checkout time, give students time to sign and write a message to the principal. Pull some magazines to have for those students that finish with their message and need something to do. A second option would be the signing could be done in conjunction with the checking out of library books. Roll or fold up the poster for easy transport. Pick two students to take the poster to the principal. Clear with the classroom teacher as other students are dismissed to return to class.

VALENTINE'S DAY LESSONS

Lesson 3

Hugs from Pearl

By Paul Schmid

Schmid, Paul. *Hugs from Pearl*. New York: Harper, 2011.

Summary: Pearl is a porcupine who loves giving hugs. Her friends enjoy getting the hugs but they are prickly. Pearl tries several things to solve her problem and eventually finds a solution.

Skills: Problem
          Solution

Grade Level: Kindergarten

Materials: Copy of the coloring sheet
          Crayons
          Pencils

Instructions: Copy the coloring sheet for all students.

Lesson

1. Introduce the title and author. Tell the students that Pearl has a problem and discuss how she solves her problem after reading the story.
2. Read the story and share the pictures.
3. Talk about the problem and solution. Pearl tried several things before getting the solution right, like, putting pincushions on her quills, cutting her quills, and taking a bath to soften the quills.
4. Move students to tables. Pass out the papers, pencils, and crayons.
5. Help students fill in the things that Pearl did to solve her problem.
6. Allow time for students to color the flowers on the sheet.

Closure: Dismiss students to check out.

How Did Pearl Solve Her Problem?

Lesson 3

Panda's Valentine's Day

By Tara Jaye Morrow

Morrow, Tara Jaye. *Panda's Valentine's Day*. New York: Sterling, 2011.

Summary: Panda and Mama usually make valentines for each other. Panda wants his valentine to look pretty, fun and show his mama's love, but he has a hard time getting finished with the valentine. He ends up throwing the incomplete valentine away.

Skills: Writing

Grade Level: First Grade

Materials: Copy of the valentine sheet
Crayons
Pencils
Wipe-off board
Markers

Instructions: Copy the valentine sheet for all students.

Lesson

1. Introduce the title and author.
2. Read the story and share the pictures.
3. Ask the students to brainstorm ideas for a valentine for a special person at their house. What words did Panda use in his mama's valentine? What words would you write in your valentine?
4. Allow time for students to complete a valentine.

Closure: Dismiss students to check out.

Write a valentine message to a special person in your life.

Lesson 3

Amelia Bedelia's First Valentine

By Herman Parish

Parish, Herman. *Amelia Bedelia's First Valentine.* New York: Greenwillow Books, 2009.

Summary: Amelia Bedelia is looking forward to the school activities that have been planned for Valentine's Day. However, she forgets her cards on the bus. At first, she is upset but discovers another way to send a greeting to each of her friends at school. She learns about cupid and even gets a bracelet from her father when she gets home from school.

Skills: Valentine's Day

Grade Level: Second Grade

Materials: Construction paper, glue, scissors, and markers

Instructions: Make copies of the five cards that Amelia makes for school. See page in the book for pictures of the valentines. It is better to make them the full size of 8-1/2 by 11 inch size construction sheet. Laminate for longer wear.

Lesson

1. Read the title and share the front cover of the book. Ask students if they have heard of Amelia Bedelia before. What is unique or special about this main character? Give students an opportunity to share other stories that they have read.
2. Read the story and stop often if the class does not understand the things that Amelia gets mixed up. Once you have explained and talked about the literal way Amelia takes things in the beginning of the book, students will start to look for others as the story progresses. Sometimes it is necessary to reread a portion again and even point out things in the illustrations. The newer books are illustrated so the pictures help explain. Do not rush the story!
3. Share with the students where the Amelia Bedelia books are located in the library since many will want to check out another story by this author.

Closure: Review how Amelia wanted to fix the valentines that the teacher had given them to use. Example: On the "Hi Heartbreaker" valentine, Amelia added a bandage across the heart. Review the other things that Amelia got mixed up in the story. Dismiss students to check out.

PRESIDENTS' DAY LESSONS

Lesson 4

Our Abe Lincoln

By Jim Aylesworth

Aylesworth, Jim. *Our Abe Lincoln.* New York: Scholastic Press, 2009.

Summary: This picture book is a remake of a Lincoln Campaign song sung to the tune of the folk song "The Old Grey Mare." The reader is introduced to Abe Lincoln as a brave, kind, wise, and honest man. Repeated phrases make it easy to follow.

Skills: Presidents' Day

Grade Level: Kindergarten

Materials: Large piece of poster board
Marker
Pictures of Lincoln and Washington from a book or magazine

Instructions: Using the song printed on the inside cover of the book, copy the words onto the poster board.

Lesson

1. Ask students what presidents' birthdays do we celebrate in the month of February. Wait for students to respond. If they are unable to give the names of Lincoln and Washington, then explain to the students. Show pictures of both the presidents. Read the title and stress that this story is about Abe Lincoln.
2. Read the text and share the pictures.
3. After the reading, ask students what kind of man was Abe Lincoln. Guide the discussion to the use of words like brave, kind, wise, and honest. These are used in the text so students should be able to recall these four characteristics. Ask for help on explaining what each mean. If students do not give an appropriate answer, help them by explaining them in terms of school-related events. For example, kindness might be helping someone who is having trouble with an art project or picking up toys after play time so that the teacher doesn't have to do it all by herself!

Closure: Show the poster and read the song to the students pointing to the words as you move through the verse. Read it a second time asking the students to help with the reading. Sing the song using the tune of "The Old Grey Mare." Let students try to sing it with you after modeling what it needs to sound like. Dismiss students to check out.

Lesson 4

What Lincoln Said

By Sarah L. Thomson

Thomson, Sarah L. *What Lincoln Said.* New York: Collins, 2009.

Summary: This book is a lighthearted account of Abe Lincoln's life. Each page includes a quote from one of his speeches. A timeline is also available in the back of the book. The illustrations show physical characteristics that Abe is well known for.

Skills: Timeline

Grade Level: First Grade

Materials: Copy of the logs
Brown construction paper
Black marker
Pencil
Scissors

Instructions: Using the copy of the logs, cut out and trace the logs onto brown construction paper. Use the black marker to add details to the logs and write the timeline items on the brown logs. See the examples for the timeline items. Cut out the logs and laminate for longer wear.

Timeline Examples

1809—Lincoln was born
1816—Family moves to Indiana
1830—Family moves to Illinois
1837—Lincoln becomes a lawyer
1842—Lincoln marries Mary Todd
1860—Lincoln becomes the president of the United States
1865—Lincoln is killed

Lesson

1. Introduce the title and author. Ask the students what they know about Abe Lincoln. Allow time for students to respond. Tell students that the pictures are going to tell what kind of house Abe Lincoln lived in, so watch carefully.

2. Read the story and share the pictures. Show the students the timeline on the last page. Ask the students if they know what a timeline is. Allow time for students to respond. Help the students out if they do not know how to answer question correctly.

3. Ask the students what kind of house Lincoln lived in. Allow time for students to respond. Show the pictures in the book that have log houses on them. Show the brown construction paper logs

that you have prepared ahead of time. Tell the students that we are going to put Lincoln's timeline in the right order.

4. Allow time for students to arrange the logs in order.

Closure: If you can find Lincoln logs, allow students to build a log cabin during checkouts.

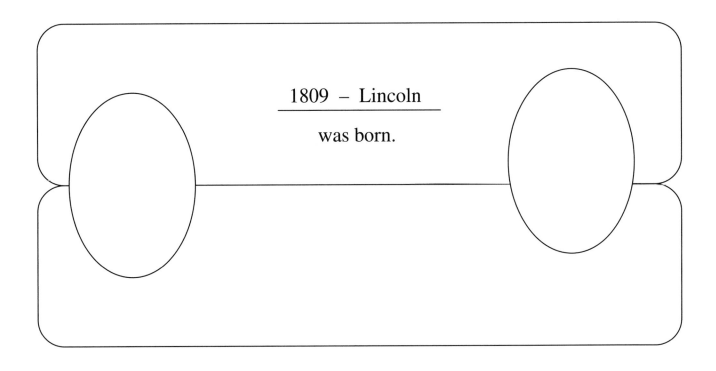

1809 – Lincoln

was born.

Lesson 4

George Washington's Birthday: A Mostly True Tale

By Margaret McNamara

McNamara, Margaret. *George Washington's Birthday: A Mostly True Tale.* New York: Schwartz & Wade Books, 2012.

Summary: This is a fiction story about George Washington's birthday. On most pages, a box appears and gives the reader the true fact or myth about George Washington. The last page includes the true facts about George in a personal narrative as if George wrote it himself.

Skills: Difference between fiction and nonfiction

Grade Level: Second Grade

Materials: A copy of the worksheet
              Overhead projector
              Chart paper
              Marker
              Pencils

Instructions: Enlarge the worksheet onto chart paper, make a transparency of the worksheet, or copy one for each student.

Lesson

1. Introduce the title and author and tell students that this is a fiction book about George Washington. The book also includes true facts about George Washington, so listen carefully and we will discuss the facts versus fiction.
2. Read the story and share the pictures and the fact and myth boxes on each page.
3. Show the worksheet either on the chart paper or overhead. Allow time for students to complete the worksheet as a group or individually if you are giving one to each student.

Closure: Read the extra page at the end of the book. Discuss the facts that were not presented in the story. Example: Names of George's brothers and sisters. General in the Revolutionary War and the first president of the United States. A different calendar was used, so George's birthday was February 11 instead of February 23. Dismiss students to check out.

Fact or Fiction

George Washington

Circle fact or fiction for each of the following statements.

FACT   **FICTION**   George cared about the weather and recorded temperatures in his diary.

FACT   **FICTION**   George did not go to school but was taught by his half-brother and a teacher near his home.

FACT   **FICTION**   George was not good at Math.

FACT   **FICTION**   George was a short man.

FACT   **FICTION**   George rode horses.

FACT   **FICTION**   Blueskin was George's favorite horse.

FACT   **FICTION**   George threw a stone across the Rappahannock River.

FACT   **FICTION**   George chopped down a cherry tree.

FACT   **FICTION**   George was a truthful man.

FACT   **FICTION**   George crossed the Delaware River many times during the war.

FACT   **FICTION**   George wore a wig.

FACT   **FICTION**   George wrote 110 rules for behavior.

FACT   **FICTION**   George always celebrated his birthday with a big party.

From *School Library Storytime: Just the Basics* written and illustrated by Brenda S. Copeland and Patricia A. Messner. Santa Barbara, CA: Libraries Unlimited. Copyright © 2013.

RESOURCES

Groundhog Day

Arno, Iris Hiskey. *The Secret of the First One Up.* Chanhassen, MN: Northword Press, 2003.

Cherry, Lynne. *How Groundhog's Garden Grew.* New York: The Blue Sky Press, 2003.

Cox, Judy. *Go to Sleep, Groundhog!* New York: Holiday House, 2004.

Cuyler, Margery. *Groundhog Stays Up Late.* New York: Walker, 2005.

Gibbons, Gail. *Groundhog Day!* New York: Holiday House, 2007.

Miller, Pat. *Substitute Groundhog.* Morton Grove, IL: Albert Whitman, 2006.

Roberts, Bethany. *Double Trouble Groundhog Day.* New York: Henry Holt, 2008.

Swallow, Pamela Curtis. *Groundhog Gets a Say.* New York: Putnam, 2005.

Valentine's Day

Carlson, Nancy L. *Henry and the Valentine Surprise.* New York: Puffin Books, 2010.

Demas, Corinne. *Valentine Surprise.* New York: Walker, 2008.

Eubank, Patti Reeder. *Valentine ABC's.* Nashville: Ideals Children's Books, 2009.

Friedman, Laurie B. *Ruby Valentine Saves the Day.* Minneapolis: Carolrhoda Books, 2010.

Gibbons, Gail. *Valentine's Day Is ...* New York: Holiday House, 2006.

Hudson, Eleanor. *The Best Thing about Valentines.* New York: Scholastic, 2004.

Novak, Matt. *My Froggy Valentine.* New Milford, CT: Roaring Brook Press, 2008.

Samuels, Barbara. *Happy Valentine's Day, Dolores.* New York: Square Fish/Farrar, Straus and Giroux, 2009.

Scieszka, Jon. *Melvin's Valentine.* New York: Aladdin, 2010.

Sutton, Benn. *Hedgehug: a Sharp Lesson in Love.* New York: Harper, 2011.

Wells, Rosemary. *Love Waves.* Somerville, MA: Candlewick Press, 2011.

100th Day

Cuyler, Margery. *100th Day Worries.* New York: Aladdin Paperbacks, 2006.

Haugen, Brenda. *The 100th Day of School.* Minneapolis: Picture Window Books, 2004.

Miller, Reagan. *100th Day of School.* New York: Crabtree, 2010.

Milord, Susan. *Happy 100th Day!* New York: Scholastic, 2011.

O'Connor, Jane. *The 100th Day of School.* New York: HarperCollins, 2009.

Presidents' Day

Hamilton, Lynn. *Presidents' Day.* New York: AV2, 2011.

Jurmain, Suzanne Tripp. *George Did It.* New York: Dutton Children's Books, 2006.

Mayer, Cassie. *Abraham Lincoln.* Chicago: Heinemann Library, 2008.

Mayer, Cassie. *George Washington.* Chicago: Heinemann Library, 2008.

Nelson, Robin. *Presidents' Day.* Minneapolis: Lerner, 2003.

Peppas, Lynn. *Presidents' Day.* New York: Crabtree, 2010.

Rabin, Staton. *Mr. Lincoln's Boys: Being the Mostly True Adventures of Abraham Lincoln's Trouble-Making Sons.* New York: Viking, 2008.

Rappaport, Doreen. *Abe's Honest Words.* New York: Hyperion Books for Children, 2008.

Rockwell, Anne. *Big George: How a Shy Boy Became President Washington.* New York: Harcourt, 2009.

St. George, Judith. *Stand Tall, Abe Lincoln.* New York: Philomel Books, 2008.

						1
2	3	**CHAPTER 7**			7	8
9	10	**MARCH**			14	15
16	17	18	19	20	21	22
23	24	25	26	27	28	29
30	31					

Many schools celebrate Dr. Seuss's birthday on March 2, so we have selected three birthday books for the library to use during this week. We have also chosen St. Patrick's Day, spring, and Music in Our Schools Month for the rest of the lessons.

BIRTHDAY LESSONS

Lesson 1

Scaredy Squirrel Has a Birthday Party

By Melanie Watt

Watt, Melanie. *Scaredy Squirrel Has a Birthday Party*. Tonawanda, New York: Kids Can Press, 2011.

Summary: Scaredy Squirrel never has big birthday parties. It is too much risk of something going wrong. It is just too risky. He decides to risk inviting a friend. See how he has to change things and the surprise he receives at the end of the story when a lot more than one show up to celebrate with him.

Skills: Birthdays

Grade Level: Second Grade

Materials: Construction paper and crayons
           Selection of Dr. Seuss books—the easier readers would be a good choice

Instructions: Cut the 8-1/2 by 11 inch sheets of construction paper in half so that each student would receive a half sheet.

Lesson

1. Read the title and share the front cover of the book. Give students time to share what was their favorite birthday party. These will vary, so limit the time for sharing. This is a topic that all will want to explain in much detail.
2. If your school is celebrating Dr. Seuss's birthday, then point out that we are partying in the library and celebrating reading by talking about birthdays. Dr. Seuss's birthday is on March 2. He is one of our favorite authors.
3. Read the story and discuss all the things that Scaredy Squirrel did to prepare for the party. Stop at each page where the party plans are illustrated and review what special events are being planned.

Closure: Booktalk some of the Dr. Seuss's books that have been pulled ahead of time. Explain where they are located on the shelf. Just like birthdays are fun and sometimes kind of crazy, Dr. Seuss has his characters doing crazy and wacky things. Dismiss students to check out.

Activity Option One: Give out Dr. Seuss books to pairs of students and let them partner read. Explain that they can move to a quiet corner, but you need to be able to see them at all times. No hiding in faraway places, behind shelves, and so on. Celebrate Dr. Seuss's birthday by reading.

Activity Option Two: Students can illustrate their favorite Dr. Seuss book jacket. Hang on the bulletin board as a display. Add some party hats to complete the display.

Lesson 1

Otis & Sydney and the Best Birthday Ever

By Laura Numeroff

Numeroff, Laura. *Otis & Sydney and the Best Birthday Ever*. New York: Abrams Books for Young Readers, 2010.

Summary: Otis and Sydney are best friends, and they always give each other a birthday party. Otis decided to plan a surprise party for Sydney. He sends out the invitations to all their friends. Otis decorates and gets ready for the party. On the day of the party, no one shows up because he put the wrong date in the invitation. Otis surprises Sydney anyway, and they celebrate together.

Skills: Comprehension

Grade Level: Kindergarten

Materials: Copy of the birthday cake
Card stock
Markers
A biography or pictures of Dr. Seuss

Instructions: Copy the birthday cake onto card stock. Using the markers, color the cakes and write the comprehension questions onto the cakes. Laminate for longer use.

Comprehension Questions

Why did Otis and Sydney become friends?
What musical instruments did they enjoy playing?
What was your favorite part?
What was your favorite picture?
Have you ever been to a surprise party? If yes, describe the party.
Describe the best birthday party you have attended.
Can you eat half a birthday cake? Why or Why not?
How many candles were on the cake?

Lesson

1. Introduce the title and author. Tell the students to listen carefully because there will be questions to answer at the end of the story.
2. Communicate to the class that the reason we are reading a birthday book is to celebrate Dr. Seuss's birthday. Share pictures from the biography of Dr. Seuss.
3. Read and share the pictures.

4. Pass out the questions to groups of two to three students. Assist each group in the reading of the question and give time for the students to collaborate on the answers.
5. Allow time for the students to share their answers with the whole class.

Closure: Dismiss students to check out.

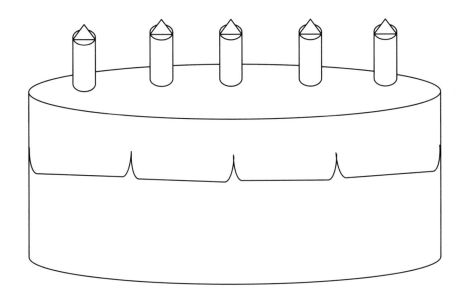

From *School Library Storytime: Just the Basics* written and illustrated by Brenda S. Copeland and Patricia A. Messner. Santa Barbara, CA: Libraries Unlimited. Copyright © 2013.

Lesson 1

Big Birthday

By Kate Hosford

Hosford, Kate. *Big Birthday*. Minneapolis: Carolrhoda Books, 2012.

Summary: Annabelle is tired of celebrating her birthday at the zoo, because she has celebrated at the zoo every year since she was four. She decides to ask her parents for a birthday on the moon. Her dad tries to suggest other possibilities. Annabelle builds a spaceship, but she can't get it off the ground. Dad helps out by hiring an astronaut. Annabelle's birthday has many issues, and finally she decides to come home. She makes plans for next year for a pirate birthday.

Skills: Extending the story

Grade Level: First Grade

Materials: Drawing paper
                Pencils
                Crayons

Lesson

1. Introduce the title and the author. Using the biography and pictures of Dr. Seuss from the kindergarten lesson, share the reason for the reading of the birthday book.
2. Read the story and share the pictures. Allow time for students to share the fun birthday activities Annabelle and her friends experienced on the moon.
3. Show the students the last picture where Annabelle is planning her next birthday. Encourage students to share ideas of what Annabelle and her friends might engage in at a pirate birthday party.
4. Pass out the drawing paper and tell students to draw a picture of a pirate birthday party after they have checked out.

Closure: Gather students together and allow time for sharing of pictures. You could make a bulletin board if need be.

ST. PATRICK'S DAY LESSONS

Lesson 2

The Night before St. Patrick's Day

By Natasha Wing

Wing, Natasha. *The Night before St. Patrick's Day*. New York: Grosset & Dunlap, 2009.

Summary: Maureen and Tim set traps all over their house so that they can catch a leprechaun. Trapping a leprechaun proves to be a hard job and finding the gold is an impossible task.

Skills: Celebration of St. Patrick's Day

Grade Level: Kindergarten

Materials: Book—*'Twas the Night before Christmas*
            Drawing paper and crayons

Lesson

1. Show the front of the book and read the title. Ask the students if they can think of another story that would have a similar title. Share the Christmas book cover so that they can make a connection before starting to read the story. Some classes will readily make the connection without showing the book while others will need a little help.
2. Read the book and share the pictures.
3. After reading the book, page through the Christmas one. Read if you have time.
4. Compare the two stories pointing out similar language and ways that the two are celebrating holidays. For example, start with the same "'Twas the night" and end with wishing the reader a Happy St. Paddy's day or a Merry Christmas. Also both stories describe either Santa or the leprechaun in the middle of the text.

Closure: Give students drawing paper and give time to draw shamrocks. Make one on the board so that students have one as a model. Dismiss students to check out.

Lesson 2

Green Shamrocks

By Eve Bunting

Bunting, Eve. *Green Shamrocks.* New York: Scholastic, 2011.

Summary: Rabbit has a packet of shamrock seeds, and he wants to plant them so that they are grown in time for the big St. Patrick's Day parade. One morning he awakens to discover that the pot of seeds is missing. Rabbit goes to all the animals in search of his missing pot.

Skills: Celebrating St. Patrick's Day

Grade Level: First Grade

Materials: Four pieces of green construction paper 8-1/2 by 11 inches
Black marker, glue, and scissors
Pictures of a squirrel, woodchuck, goat, rabbit

Instructions: Cut out pictures of a squirrel, woodchuck, goat, and rabbit. Old magazines or coloring books are good places to find these animals. Glue one to each of the green paper. Write the name of the animal underneath each picture. Decorate with shamrocks if you wish.

Lesson

1. Open by asking students if they have ever lost something. Ask them what do they have to do to find the lost object? Explain that the main character in the story loses something and has to figure out who took the shamrocks. Sometimes you have to get help from other people to find the object that you lost. Listen for the helpers in the story.
2. Read the book and share the pictures.
3. Review with the students the steps that the rabbit took to get his shamrocks planted: found a pot, filled the pot with dirt, sowed the seeds, watered the seeds, and moved the pot to make sure it had both sun and shade.
4. Ask if they noticed any characters that helped the rabbit out in the story. Let students name these animals.

Closure: Lay out the four animal pictures so all students can see them easily. Ask: "Which of the four characters is the story about?" The students should point out that the rabbit is the one that the story is about. Explain that the rabbit is on each page and he is the one doing the action. He is the main character. Stress that others help the rabbit complete the story. We call these characters the supporting characters. Dismiss students to check out.

Lesson 2

The Leprechaun Who Lost His Rainbow

By Sean Callahan

Callahan, Sean. *The Leprechaun Who Lost His Rainbow.* Morton Grove, IL: Albert Whitman & Company, 2009.

Summary: Roy G. Biv has lost his rainbow and enlists the help of Colleen to get the rainbow back. Colleen has to give something of hers for every color to make the rainbow—licorice for red, basketball for orange, and so on. Mr. Biv says that she has to give up her most priced penny whistle for the green color. Colleen's grandfather brought the whistle to her from Ireland. In the end, Colleen gives her penny whistle up and in return is rewarded with a silver flute. Information about rainbows and Roy G. Biv is located in the back of the book.

Skills: Connecting text to self

Grade Level: Second Grade

Materials: Copy of the worksheet
Pencils
Crayons
Wipe-off board
Marker

Instructions: Copy the worksheet for each student.

Lesson

1. Introduce the title and author. Ask the students if they know the colors in the rainbow. Allow time for students to respond. Write the responses on the wipe-off board.
2. Read the story and share the pictures. Discuss the colors of the rainbow and edit the list that was made earlier. Ask the students the items that Annabelle gave to bring the rainbow back. Write the name of the item next to the color.
3. Pass out a worksheet and a pencil to each student. Read the directions and explain to the students that they will need to color the rainbow and write what items they would give up for the rainbow. Students can complete this during checkout times.
4. Dismiss students to check out.
5. Allow time for students to check out and complete the worksheet.

Closure: Gather students back together to share their rainbow worksheets. Share the last page about rainbows and Roy G. Biv.

What would you give up for a rainbow?

Color the rainbow with the correct colors and write what you would give for the rainbow on the lines below the rainbow.

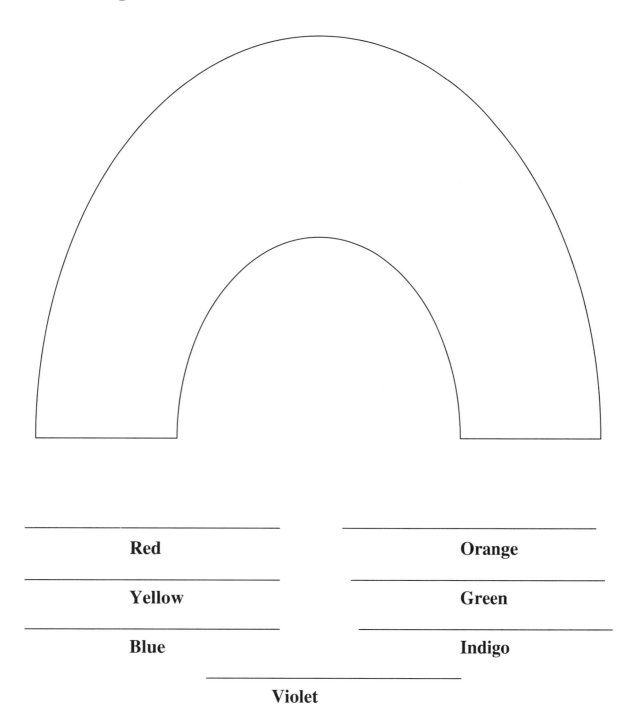

_____	_____
Red	**Orange**
_____	_____
Yellow	**Green**
_____	_____
Blue	**Indigo**

_____

Violet

Lesson 3

Are You Ready for Spring?

By Shelia Anderson

Anderson, Shelia. *Are You Ready for Spring?* Minneapolis: Lerner, 2010.

Summary: Informational book about spring that includes sights, sounds, and weather. Also previewed are things to look forward to when spring is over and summer arrives.

Skills: Signs of spring

Grade Level: Kindergarten

Materials: Collection of pictures that would represent things used and seen in both winter and spring. Example: Mittens, snowman, sled, and winter jacket might be for winter. Rain boots, bird in a nest, umbrella, and seeds would be items for spring
Colored pieces of construction paper, glue, and scissors

Instructions: Mount the pictures on separate pieces of paper.

Lesson

1. Greet students, show the cover, and point to the words as you read the title. Ask what season of the year has just passed. Lead the students in a discussion about winter and then the arrival of a new season called spring. Explain that we are going to read a nonfiction book about spring. Students should listen for all the signs of spring that the book highlights.
2. Read the story. Stop before reading some of the pages and ask students to picture-read. Ask questions: What is happening now? Have you seen this outside? For example, the picture of the bird on a nest. Ask if students have noticed any birds outside.

Closure: Spread the pictures out for all students to see. Explain that some are signs of spring and others we would see or use during the winter season. Select a quiet student to come pick out one for spring. Move though the pictures alternating spring and then winter until all the pictures have been discussed. Dismiss students to check out.

Lesson 3

Fletcher and the Springtime Blossoms

By Julia Rawlinson

Rawlinson, Julia. *Fletcher and the Springtime Blossoms*. New York: Greenwillow Books, 2009.

Summary: Fletcher the fox loves everything about the spring morning. However, when he sees white snowy flakes falling from the branches in the orchard, he is worried that snow must be coming and it will be too cold for his friends. Racing off to warn his friends, they soon discover that Fletcher's snow is really blossoms falling from the trees. Celebrate the coming of spring with Fletcher and his forest friends.

Skills: Celebration of spring

Grade Level: First Grade

Materials: Large poster paper, scrap construction paper, crayons, glue, scissors, and markers

Instructions: Cut a long length of white paper big enough for a mural scene that lots of students can work around.

Lesson

1. Ask students to help create a list of signs of spring. Write them on the board as they call out the answers. These should include warmer weather, flowers coming up, butterflies and birds returning.
2. Read the title of the story and explain that Fletcher the fox loves springtime.
3. After the reading, review the signs of spring that the students might have noticed in the story. Compare with the list on the board.

Closure: Show the poster and explain that the library class is going to create a mural of spring. Point out that they can draw and cut out items to go on the mural. Refer to the list that they made in the beginning. Remind students that Fletcher and his friends need to be part of the mural. Divide up the class, and let half the class create items to glue on to the mural while the other students color and draw the grass and trees as a background. Dismiss students to check out.

Lesson 3

Stuck

By Oliver Jeffers

Jeffers, Oliver. *Stuck*. New York: Philomel Books, 2011.

Summary: Floyd gets his kite stuck in a tree. He tries throwing different things at the tree to release the kite. He even tries the kitchen sink. After trying a while, the kite falls out and Floyd enjoys the rest of his day flying his kite. He goes to bed thinking that he has forgotten something, like all the things that are still in the tree.

Skills: Predicting
Problem
Solution
Sequencing

Grade Level: Second Grade

Materials: Copy of the kite pattern
Markers
Bright-colored card stock
Yarn
Scarps of paper

Instructions: Copy the kite pattern onto the cards stock and cut out. Write the things that Floyd threw at the tree on the kites, one item for each kite. Examples: One shoe, other shoe, cat. Laminate for longer wear. You can add a kite tail using the yarn and scrap paper.

Lesson

1. Introduce the title and author. Ask the students if they know what predicting means. Allow time for students to explain; if they don't have a clue, explain that predicting is when you state what you think will happen next. Tell the students that there are a couple of places in the book that they can predict what happens next.
2. Read the story and stop on the two pages where Floyd tosses the ladder and saw at the tree and ask the students what they think will happen next. Allow time for responses.
3. Ask the students about the problem and solution. Allow time for students to respond.

Closure: Allow time for students to sequence the kites in the order they appeared in the story. Dismiss students to check out.

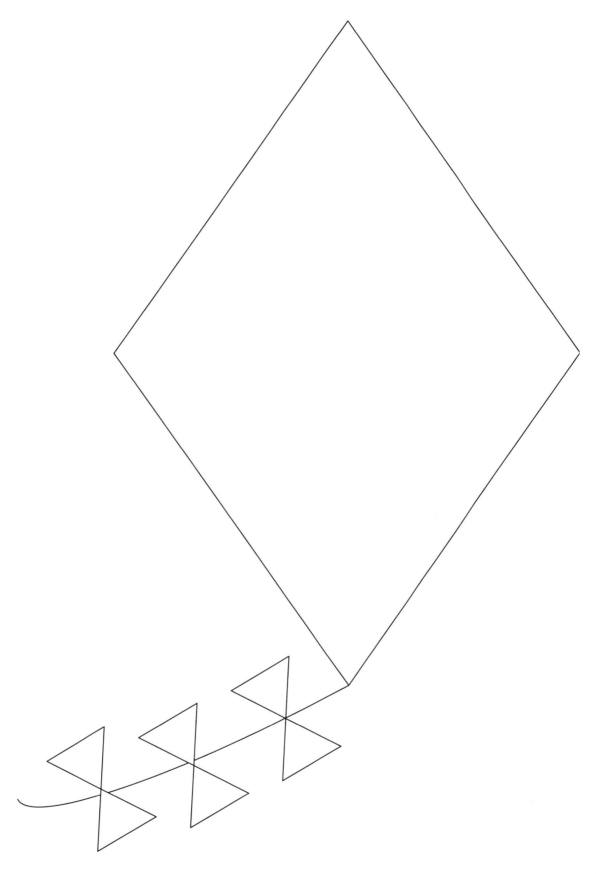

From *School Library Storytime: Just the Basics* written and illustrated by Brenda S. Copeland and Patricia A. Messner. Santa Barbara, CA: Libraries Unlimited. Copyright © 2013.

MUSIC LESSONS

Lesson 4

Just a Little Music

By Mercer Mayer

Meyer, Mercer. *Just a Little Music.* New York: Harper Festival, 2010.

Summary: After watching a parade, Little Critter wants to play music. He and his dad visit a music store to pick out the right one for Little Critter. Each instrument is tried until the drums are decided as the perfect match. No one at home likes his practice sessions, and they decide that maybe he needs lessons.

Skills: Music month

Grade Level: Kindergarten

Materials: Pictures of musical instruments found in the story: tuba, flute, trombone, guitar, and drums
Construction paper, scissors, and glue
Musical CD

Instructions: Cut out the instruments and mount on the construction paper.

Lesson

1. Explain as you begin story hour that this is the month we celebrate music. Show the cover of the book and read the title.
2. Ask the students to predict what they think will happen in the story by looking at the front cover. Give time for answers.
3. Read the story and share the pictures. Talk about how Little Critter felt when he picked out an instrument to play. Then ask about how his sister and parents felt about all the loud noise?

Closure: Lay out the instruments and ask students to name each one. Talk about those that would have a deep sound and those that would have a high pitch. Ask for a volunteer to make the sound that they think each would make. Rotate around the room giving different students the chance to imitate the sounds. Play music softly while students make their book selection. Dismiss students to check out.

Lesson 4

Dancing with the Dinosaurs

By Jane Clarke

Clarke, Jane. *Dancing with the Dinosaurs.* Watertown, MA: An Imagine Book, 2012.

Summary: All the different kinds of dinosaurs are in a dance contest. There are even judges like the ones on the television show "Dancing with the Stars." Each dinosaur dances a different kind of dance until it is time for dinner, and they rush from the room.

Skills: Critical thinking
       Addition

Grade Level: First Grade

Materials: Card stock
       Copy of the numbers
       Copy of the tally sheet
       Chart paper
       Marker

Instructions: Copy the numbers onto card stock, cut apart, and laminate. You will need numbers 0–5 for each student. Enlarge the tally sheet for each class onto chart paper.

Lesson

1. Ask the students if they have ever seen the television show *Dancing with the Stars*. Allow time for students to share. Introduce the title and author and tell the class that this book is similar to the show, but it has dinosaurs. Also, tell the class that after the reading, they will be judges and can vote for their favorite dinosaur, best costumes, and the best dance. You might have to explain the concept of rating to the kids and give some examples, particularly if they have not seen that show on television.
2. Read the story and share the pictures.
3. Pass out the numbers and explain to the students that they will need to give a number to each of the dinosaurs, 0 being the lowest and 5 the highest. Think about the kind of dinosaur, costume, and dance.
4. Show the pictures again to the students and have them put up a number like a real judge.
5. Record the students' numbers onto the enlarged tally sheet.
6. Tally each of the columns and announce the winner of "Dancing with the Dinosaurs."

Closure: Dismiss students to check out.

0	1
2	3
4	5

From *School Library Storytime: Just the Basics* written and illustrated by Brenda S. Copeland and Patricia A. Messner. Santa Barbara, CA: Libraries Unlimited. Copyright © 2013.

T. Rex	Steggy	Duckbills	Raptors	Troodie	Saurus	Tops	Barry	Kylie	Maia	Spike	Donny	Breakers	Lily	All-saur

Lesson 4

Rock 'N' Roll Mole

By Carolyn Crimi

Crimi, Carolyn. *Rock 'N' Roll Mole.* New York: Dial Books for Young Readers, 2011.

Summary: Mole is a guitar player with lots of soul. He wears a leather jacket and shades at night. Mole does not play in public and Pig tries to get him to play in the talent show. Mole agrees to help get ready for the talent show but not to play. Pig tries one last time to get Mole to play by telling Mole that his iPod was broken. Mole runs home and gets his guitar and plays for the talent show.

Skills: Problem
       Solution

Grade Level: Second Grade

Materials: Chart paper
       Marker

Instructions: Make a poster that reads "Talent Show." Hang the poster so all students can view. Research the famous musicians and find pictures or music that you can share after the reading of the story.

Lesson

1. Introduce the title and author, by showing the front cover of the book. Tell the students that March is music in the school's month, and the book for today has a music theme. Ask the students to listen for three musicians whose names sound like famous musicians. Tell them this story has a problem and a solution.
2. Read the story and share the pictures. Ask students about the three musicians and show the pages where they appear in the book. The musicians are Mick Badger, Goose Springsteen, and Moo2. Tell the students about the famous musicians who have similar names.
3. Talk about the problem and the solution. Allow time for students to share the details of how Pig solved the problem.
4. Lead a discussion on what kind of talent everyone has in the class. Allow time for students to share. Dismiss students to check out.

RESOURCES

Birthday/Dr. Seuss

Bruel, Nick. *Happy Birthday Bad Kitty.* New York: Roaring Brook Press, 2010.

Carlson, Cheryl. *Dr. Seuss.* Mankato, MN: Capstone Press, 2005.

Huget, Jennifer LaRue. *The Best Birthday Party Ever.* New York: Random House, 2011.

St. Patrick's Day

Callahan, Sean. *Shannon and the World's Tallest Leprechaun.* Morton Grove, IL: Whitman, 2008.

DePaola, Tomie. *Fin M'Coul: The Giant of Knockmany Hill.* New York: Holiday House, 1981.

Goeller, Dorothy. *St. Patrick's Day.* Berkeley Heights, NJ: Bailey Books, 2011.

Rockwell, Anne F. *St. Patrick's Day.* New York: Harper, 2010.

Slater, Teddy. *The Luckiest St. Patrick's Day Ever!* New York: Scholastic, 2007.

Spring

Amoroso, Cynthia. *Spring.* Mankato, MN: Child's World, 2010.

Na, Il Sung. *Snow Rabbit, Spring Rabbit: A Book of Changing Seasons.* New York: Alfred A. Knopf, 2010.

Music

Alexander, Kwame. *Acoustic Rooster and His Barnyard Band.* Ann Arbor, MI: Sleeping Bear Press, 2011.

Bechdolt, Jack. *Little boy with a Big Horn.* New York: A Golden Book, 2008.

Benjamin, Floella. *My Two Grandads.* London: Frances Lincoln Childrens' Books, 2010.

Busse, Sarah Martin. *Banjo Granny.* Boston: Houghton Mifflin, 2006.

Falconer, Ian. *Olivia Forms a Band.* New York: Atheneum Books for Young Readers, 2006.

		1	2	3	4	5
6	7				11	12
13	14				18	19
20	21	22	23	24	25	26
27	28	29	30			

CHAPTER 8

APRIL

April has a wide variety of special days, weeks, and monthlong celebrations. We chose April Fool's Day, Baseball Opening Day, Planting a Garden, and Easter for the lessons in this group. April is also National Frog Month and National Poetry Month. Other special days and weeks are Pet Owners' Day, Earth Day, National Arbor day, and National Library Week. Eileen Christelow celebrates her birthday on April 22.

APRIL FOOL'S LESSONS

Lesson 1

April Fool! Watch Out at School!

By Diane deGroat

deGroat, Diane. *April Fool! Watch Out at School!* New York: HarperCollins, 2009.

Summary: Gilbert is anxious to play tricks on his friends at school, but he is the one that everyone is playing tricks on. Lewis, the bully, is the worse prankster of all. Will Gilbert be able to play a trick on him by the end of the story? The illustrator has played some tricks with the illustrations so the students will enjoy finding all the mistakes.

Skills: April Fool's Day

Grade Level: Kindergarten

Lesson

1. Open the discussion with talk about April Fool's Day. Ask if students are ready to play tricks on their friends. Talk about what is an appropriate trick. If it harms another friend, then it is not a good trick. For example, playing a trick that would cause a friend to fall.

2. Before reading the story, explain that the illustrator has made tricks in the drawings and that they might want to look for them as you move along. Ask them to keep them a secret until after the story is read. You can then go back to the beginning and see what is wrong on each page. Check the copyright page for a list of mistakes. This will make it easier to guide the students through the process.

Closure: Ask students if they enjoyed the way the illustrator tried to trick them. Dismiss students to check out.

Lesson 1

April Fool, Phyllis!

By Susanna Leonard Hill

Hill, Susanna Leonard. *April Fool, Phyllis.* New York: Holiday House, 2011.

Summary: Phyllis feels like winter is not over even though the calendar says April 1, and it still feels like snow is coming. Will they be able to have the spring treasure hunt anyway?

Skills: April Fool's Day

Grade Level: First Grade

Materials: Paper and marker

Instructions: Create clues for a treasure hunt in the library.

For Example

Clue 1: Go to the place where we place our books after we check them in. Answer: Book cart. Hide the second clue under the shelf so the students do not see it when they check in the books

Clue 2: This is the location of something that helps us keep our place while we decide if we are taking a book home. Answer: Shelf markers

Clue 3: Where do we sign out books? Answer: Circulation desk

Clue 4: Where would we locate fact books about spring? Answer: Nonfiction

    Hide an assortment of stickers where the last clue is located.

Lesson

1. Share the title of the book and ask the students to explain what April fool means. Give time for students to share. Each group may be different, so be prepared to explain what people do on this day and give an example.
2. Read the story and share the pictures.

Closure: Prepare the students for a treasure hunt by reviewing the events of the story. Explain that we will have our own spring treasure hunt and read the first clue. Help them decide where the next clue would be hidden. When the stickers are found, explain that the weather books would be located in this area of the library. Pull off a spring book and a snow book to share with the group. Dismiss students to check out.

Lesson 1

The Library Pages

By Carlene Morten

Morten, Carlene. *The Library Pages.* Madison, WI: UpstartBooks, 2010.

Summary: Mrs. Heath, the regular Librarian, is away from Happyland Elementary School Library. Her substitute appoints some Library Pages to help in the library. The Library Pages decide to make a DVD of what they are doing to help and send it to Mrs. Heath. The only problem is, it seems, they created a mess instead of helping. At the end of the DVD, they scream "April Fool." This is a delightful reminder of good manners in the library.

Skills: April Fool's Day

Grade Level: Second Grade

Materials: Poster paper and marker

Instructions: Label the poster with "Disasters at Happyland Elementary School Library."

Lesson

1. Share the front cover of the book. Ask students to listen for all the things that the helpers do at the library.
2. After reading the story, ask the students if they were surprised at the helpers screaming "April Fool" at the end of the book.

Closure: Make a list of all the things that should not happen at the library as pointed out in the story. Dismiss students to check out.

a. Putting all the skinny books together
b. Color coding the nonfiction books
c. Taking the books to lunch
d. Do not use duct tape on repairs. Needs to be special library tape
e. The spines need to be showing outward
f. Using a pencil as a bookmarker
g. Taking books to the playground
h. Coloring in the illustrations

EASTER LESSONS

Lesson 2

Ollie's Easter Egg

By Olivier Dunrea

Dunrea, Olivier. *Ollie's Easter Egg.* Boston: Houghton Mifflin, 2009.

Summary: Ollie is a little gosling that is watching the eggs being dyed and hidden for the Easter Egg hunt. Ollie decides that all of the eggs are for him, and no one seems to be able to find them.

Skills: Easter

Grade Level: Kindergarten

Lesson

1. Show the title of the story and ask if any of the students have taken part in an egg hunt. Give time for sharing but watch the time because many will want to take part. Lots of students will be able to connect with this story.
2. Read the story and share the pictures as you move through the text.

Closure: As students select books, help students locate other spring and Easter stories. If you have them labeled with a special spine sticker, be sure to share at this time.

Lesson 2

Peepsqueak!

By Leslie Ann Clark

Clark, Leslie Ann. *Peepsqueak!* New York: Harper, 2012.

Summary: Peepsqueak wants to fly high, but all the animals tell him that he is too little to fly high. He tries many things but nothing works. At last, Old Gray Goose takes Peepsqueak high in the sky. This book is full of repetitive words and a great read aloud.

Skills: Audience participation

Grade Level: First Grade

Materials: Wipe-off board
Markers

Instructions: Write the word "He was on the move!" and "up, up, up" and "down, down, down" on the wipe-off board.

Lesson

1. Introduce the title and author. Show the students the words on the board and practice reading the words as you point to the letters. Tell the students that they will need to help with the story, by repeating the words on the board when they appear in the story.
2. Read the story and point to the words as they appear in the story. Students love this story because there are many places for them to join in the reading.

Closure: Dismiss students to check out.

Lesson 2

The Easter Egg

By Jan Brett

Brett, Jan. *The Easter Egg.* New York: G.P. Putnam's Sons, 2010.

Summary: Every year the bunny that decorates the winning egg in the contest gets to help the Easter bunny hide the eggs on Easter morning. Hoppi has never decorated an egg before, but he is hoping to have the winning egg.

Skills: Easter

Grade Level: Second Grade

Materials: White construction paper, crayons, pencils, and scissors
A selection of Jan Brett books

Instructions: Cut the 8-1/2 by 11 inch paper into half sheets so that each student can have a sheet.

Lesson

1. Share the front cover of the book and read the title and author. Many second graders will recognize this popular author. See if they can name other books written by Jan Brett.
2. Hold up some that you have pulled ahead of time that are written by this author. Ask for a thumbs-up if they have read that book.
3. Read the book and share the pictures. Talk about how Jan Brett adds extras into her illustrations. Point out the robins at the top of each page. The robins are a big part of this story. Also note the eggs and scenes that are on the sides of each page.

Closure: Pass out paper and give students an opportunity to create their own Easter egg. Remind them that they need to be big enough to cut out. The egg should be as big as their outstretched hand. Ask them to draw the egg in pencil before using crayons in case they make the egg too small on the first try. Collect and hang the eggs on the bulletin board. Dismiss students to check out.

BASEBALL LESSONS

Lesson 3

Quacky Baseball

By Peter Abrahams

Abrahams, Peter. *Quacky Baseball.* New York: Harper, 2011.

Summary: Thumby Duckling is playing baseball for the first time with the Webbies on opening day. He is really nervous but does his part to help the team win. He catches a fly ball and hits a home run in the ninth inning.

Skills: Connecting text to self
Nonfiction

Grade Level: Kindergarten

Materials: Baseball hat
Baseball jersey
Baseball glove
Baseball

Instructions: Gather baseball equipment and clothing for a costume. Wear the costume for the class as they enter the library.

Lesson

1. Ask the students what the book will be about today? Another question might be: Does anyone play baseball on a team? Or do you play in the yard with your mom, your dad, or brothers and sisters?
2. Introduce the author and title. Tell the students that this book is a fiction book, but it has a few nonfiction facts about baseball. Listen for the facts, and we will talk about them at the end of the story.
3. Read the story and share the pictures.
4. Ask the students if they remember any of the nonfiction facts. Page back through the book and show the students the pages that have the facts on them.

Closure: Show the students the nonfiction books about baseball and dismiss them to check out books.

Lesson 3

Daddy Adventure Day

By Dave Keane

Keane, Dave. *Daddy Adventure Day*. New York: Philomel, 2011.

Summary: Daddy and the little boy spend the day with each other as a daddy adventure day. Daddy cannot read his newspaper or talk on his cell phone. They go to the ballpark for the little boy's first baseball game. The little boy spills hot chocolate and root beer on Daddy. Even though the day is messy, their team wins, and they enjoyed the daddy adventure day.

Skills: Connecting text to self

Grade Level: First Grade

Materials: Baseball costume from kindergarten lesson

Instructions: Wear the costume as you greet the students.

Lesson

1. Greet the students in the baseball costume. Ask the students if they have ever been to a baseball game. Allow time for students to share. Another question might be: Has anyone been to a major league baseball game? Allow time for students to share.
2. Introduce the title and author. Tell the students to listen carefully and we will talk about the baseball game that the little boy went to in the story.
3. Read the story and share the pictures.
4. Lead a discussion on the events that took place at the ballpark. Examples: Buying souvenirs, singing and chanting, and eating. Allow time for students to share their favorite souvenirs and foods.

Closure: Dismiss students to check out.

Lesson 3

Clorinda Plays Baseball!

By Robert Kinerk

Kinerk, Robert. *Clorinda Plays Baseball!* New York: Simon & Schuster Books for Young Readers, 2012.

Summary: Clorinda, the cow, wants to play for the Red Hats a big league team in Bosstown. She can hit and throw the ball really far, but can't seem to get to the big league. Deke, a young boy, appears and wants to learn how to play ball. Clorinda teaches him all she knows. The scouts come and sign Deke to the Red Hats. Clorinda is sad, but helps coach Deke. A sandstorm allows Clorinda to punch hit for Deke and her dream of playing in the big leagues comes true.

Skills: Connecting self to text

Grade Level: Second Grade

Materials: Costume for previous lessons

Instructions: Wear the costume as you greet the students

Lesson

1. Begin by asking the question: Has anyone ever dreamed of playing baseball for a professional team? Allow time for students to respond and also talk about any professional teams that might be in your area.
2. Introduce the title and author and tell the students that Clorinda is dreaming of playing for the big leagues.
3. Read the story and share the pictures. The pictures are loaded with details, so take your time and make sure that children pore over the pages. This book is illustrated by Steven Kellogg—his books have lots of details.

Closure: Dismiss students to check out.

GARDEN LESSONS

Lesson 4

My Garden

By Kevin Henkes

Henkes, Kevin. *My Garden.* New York: Greenwillow, 2010.

Summary: A young girl helps her mother water, weed, and take care of the garden. Then she starts to imagine her own dream garden, silly and full of youthful imagination.

Skills: Gardening

Grade Level: Kindergarten

Lesson

1. Share the title and author of the story. Ask the students to predict what kind of garden the little girl is talking about.
2. Read the story and enjoy the dream with the kids as the story unfolds.

Closure: Close by letting the students share what kind of garden they would plant. What kind of flowers or vegetables would they have been growing in their garden? Dismiss students to check out.

Lesson 4

The Imaginary Garden

By Andrew Larsen

Larsen, Andrew. *The Imaginary Garden*. Tonawanda, NY: Kids Can Press, 2009.

Summary: When Poppa moves to an apartment, his gardening days are over. But his granddaughter Theo has a wonderful idea of painting a garden using paints and brushes, in other words an imaginary garden. The result is a masterpiece and lots of joy as they carefully add each flower and brushstroke.

Skills: Gardening

Grade Level: First Grade

Lesson

1. All first graders love to play in the dirt, and they will relate to the idea of gardening.
2. Before reading, ask: What kind of things do we grow in gardens? Give time for students to respond.
3. After the reading, review the steps that Poppa and Theo did to complete their imaginary garden. These should include: plan the garden out on paper first, start with a wall for the back on the garden, paint in the soil, and then add the plants and flowers.

Closure: Dismiss students to check out.

Lesson 4

The Goodbye Cancer Garden

By Janna Matties

Matties, Janna. *The Goodbye Cancer Garden*. Chicago: Albert Whitman & Company, 2011.

Summary: Janie and Jeffrey hear the sad news from their dad that their mom has cancer. After lots of questions to the doctor, they decide to plant a garden because the doctor said by pumpkin time, Mom should feel better. They plan and plant the garden and watch it grow. By pumpkin-picking time, Mom is better, and they make their own pumpkin bread and roast the seeds to enjoy. This is a real celebration of family and the healing powers of love.

Skills: Gardening

Grade Level: Second Grade

Lesson

1. Be sure to read this powerful story ahead of time because it may spark a lot of questions and it is best to know how you want to lead the discussion.
2. Read the book and share the pictures. Start the discussion time by asking: How did the garden help this family?

Closure: Make a list on the board of the things that they needed to do to plant the garden. The list should include dig up the vegetable bed, draw a map of the layout, pick out the seeds, visit a garden shop, plant, weed, and water. Dismiss students to check out.

RESOURCES

April Fool's Day

Bateman, Teresa. *April Foolishness.* Morton Grove, IL: Albert Whitman & Co., 2004.

Brown, Marc Tolon. *Arthur's April Fool.* New York: Little, Brown, 1983.

McMullan, Kate. *Pearl and Wagner: One Funny Day.* New York: Dial Books for Young Readers, 2009.

Welling, Peter J. *Michael le Souffle' and the April Fool.* Gretna, LA: Pelican Pub., 2003.

Easter

Grambling, Lois G. *Here Comes T. Rex Cottontail.* New York: Katherine Tegen Books, 2007.

Mortimer, Anne. *Bunny's Easter Egg.* New York: Katherine Tegen books, 2010.

Stoeke, Janet Morgan. *Minerva Louise and the Colorful Eggs.* New York: Puffin Books, 2008.

Thomas, Jan. *Here Comes the Big, Mean Dust Bunny!* New York: Beach Lane Books, 2009.

Thomas, Jan. *Rhyming Dust Bunnies.* New York: Beach Lane Books, 2009.

Wallace, Carol. *Easter Bunny Blue.* New York: Holiday House, 2009.

Garden

Aliki. *Quiet in the Garden.* New York: Greenwillow Books, 2009.

George, Lindsay Barrett. *In the Garden: Who's Been There?* New York: Greenwillow Books, 2006.

Gunzi, Christine. *Who's Hiding?: In the Garden.* Hauppauge, NY: Barron's, 2010.

Schuh, Mari C. *Tools for the Garden.* Mankato, MN: Capstone Press, 2010.

Wilson, Karma. *Mortimer's First Garden.* New York: Margaret K. McElderry Books, 2009.

Baseball

Biedrzycki, David. *Ace Lacewing, Bug Detective: The Big Swat.* Watertown, MA: Charlesbridge, 2010.

Crowe, Chris. *Just as Good: How Larry Doby Changed America's Game.* Somerville, MA: Candlewick Press, 2012.

Gantos, Jack and Nicole Rubel. *Three Strikes for Rotten Ralph.* New York: Farrar Straus Giroux, 2011.

Krensky, Stephen. *Play Ball, Jackie.* Minneapolis: Millbrook Press, 2011.

Lester, Helen. *Batter up Wombat.* Boston: Houghton Mifflin, 2006.

Lies, Brian. *Bats at the Ballgame.* Boston: Houghton Mifflin Books for Children, 2010.

Newman, Jeff. *The Boys.* New York: Simon & Schuster Books for Young Readers, 2010.

Van Dusen, Chris. *Randy Riley's Really Big Hit.* Somerville, MA: Candlewick Press, 2012.

Wheeler, Lisa. *Dino-baseball.* Minneapolis: Carolrhoda Books, 2010.

				1	2	3
4	5				9	10
11	12				16	17
18	19	20	21	22	23	24
25	26	27	28	29	30	31

CHAPTER 9

MAY

Mother's Day, flowers, zoo animals, and vacations are highlighted in the May lessons. Other special days are Mother Goose Day, Cinco de Mayo, and Memorial Day. The featured author is Don Wood, who has a birthday on May 4.

MOTHER'S DAY LESSONS

Lesson 1

Mother's Day Surprise

By Stephen Krensky

Krensky, Stephen. *Mother's Day Surprise.* Tarrytown, NY: Marshall Cavendish Children, 2010.

Summary: Violet the snake enjoys being with her friends and plays during free time. Things change when spring arrives. All the other animals are too busy to play because they are making something for their moms for Mother's Day. Violet has a hard time coming up with a surprise for her mom. All the things that her friends are doing are too hard for her to do.

Skills: Mother's Day

Grade Level: Kindergarten

Lesson

1. Start the storytime by asking the students if they ever do anything special for their moms. Give time for student interaction. Explain that today's story is about a snake that wants to do something special but can't decide what she can do best.
2. Read the story and share the illustrations.

Closure: Ask students to explain what each animal made for their mom. These should include fox, skunk, squirrel, bear, and beaver. Ask: Why was Violet not able to do the same things the other animals were able to do? Was the gift that Violet gave her mom appropriate for her? Dismiss students to check out.

Lesson 1

T. Rex and the Mother's Day Hug

By Lois G. Grambling

Grambling, Lois G. *T. Rex and the Mother's Day Hug.* New York: Katherine Tegen Books, 2008.

Summary: T. Rex never buys anything for his mom for Mother's Day. He always wants to do something that is extra special. His mom says that she just wants a hug. T. Rex decides to make over her car.

Skills: Mother's Day

Grade Level: First Grade

Materials: A sheet of paper for each student, crayons, and markers

Instructions: Cut each sheet into half so students can fold and make a card.

Lesson

1. Introduce the story by asking if the students are making their moms something for Mother's Day. Often the classroom teacher has a project planned, and this can be a good way for the students to share what they are working on.
2. Point out that today's story is about T. Rex, who wants to do something extra special for his mom.
3. Read the story and stop at different points in the story to ask for predictions. Build up the excitement to the end of the story.

Closure: Stress that often our moms like to get special cards and artwork for holidays. Pass out the sheets and crayons. Give students time to create a card for their mom. Write on the board any words that they might have trouble spelling. Some might include happy, Mother's Day, special, and love. Dismiss students to check out.

Lesson 1

Fancy Nancy: Ooh La La! It's Beauty Day

By Jane O'Connor

O'Connor, Jane. *Fancy Nancy: Ooh La La! It's Beauty Day.* New York: Harper, 2010.

Summary: Fancy Nancy's mom and dad are going out to celebrate her mom's birthday. Fancy Nancy wants to pamper her mom and give her a spa day so she can look great for the special dinner. The spa is set up in the backyard, but a problem arises. What will she do to get the mess straightened out?

Skills: Mother's Day

Grade Level: Second Grade

Materials: Poster paper and marker

Lesson

1. Read the title and author. Ask a student to show where the Fancy Nancy books are located in the library. Review that the author's last name starts with the letter "O," so all of the other Fancy Nancy books are located in the same spot on the O shelf.
2. Read the story and stop often to compare the fancy words with the ordinary words. For example, "pamper" is the fancy word for spoiling. As you come across these words, write them on the poster paper.

Closure: Review the words that are on the list. Use them to review the main points of the story. Dismiss students to check out.

Lesson 2

Floop's Flowers

By Carole Tremblay

Tremblay, Carole. *Floop's Flowers*. New York: Alphabet Soup, 2010.

Summary: Floop invites friends over for a snack. He makes a yummy feast and wants to decorate the table with flowers. He goes outside to gather flowers and gets sidetracked by rolling in the green grass, leaping over stones, observing a butterfly, smelling a flower, and playing with ants.

Skills: Sequencing

Grade Level: Kindergarten

Materials: Flower pattern
Bright-colored construction paper
Marker
Basket

Instructions: Copy the flower pattern onto the colored construction paper. Write one event from the story on each flower. Laminate, cut out, and place in the basket.

Events: Floop invites his friends over.
Floop makes a yummy feast.
Floop decorates his table.
Floop rolls in the green grass.
Floop leaps over stones.
Floop observes a butterfly.
Floop smells a flower.
Floop plays with an ant.
Floop picks one flower.

Lesson

1. Introduce the title and author. Ask the students if they have seen flowers growing in their yards. Allow time for students to share. Tell students that sometimes people pick flowers out of their yards and arrange them for their table. Floop in the story does that very thing.
2. Read the story and share the pictures.
3. Show the basket with the flowers and assist the students in sequencing the events in the story.

Closure: Dismiss students to check out.

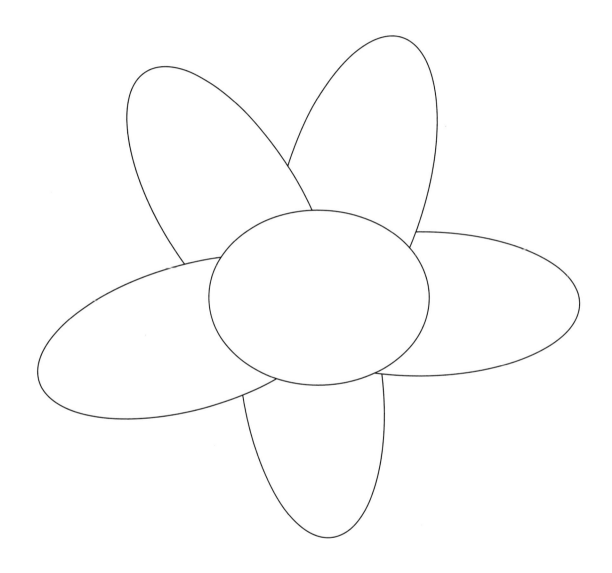

From *School Library Storytime: Just the Basics* written and illustrated by Brenda S. Copeland and Patricia A. Messner. Santa Barbara, CA: Libraries Unlimited. Copyright © 2013.

Lesson 2

Huck Runs Amuck!

By Sean Taylor

Taylor, Sean. *Huck Runs Amuck!* New York: Dial Books for Young Readers, 2011.

Summary: Huck will eat almost anything, like boxes, gloves, or birds' nests, but he loves to eat flowers. This story takes Huck all over the place with many encounters with flowers. After every encounter, the reader will wonder: Where will Huck find flowers next?

Skills: Sequencing

Grade Level: First Grade

Materials: Flower pattern from kindergarten lesson
Bright-colored construction paper
Marker
Basket

Instructions: Copy the flower pattern onto the colored construction paper. Write in one place Huck found flowers from the story on each flower. Laminate, cut out, and place in the basket.

Places: Skinny Mountain
Clothesline
Mr. Watson's flowers
Mrs. Spooner's hat
Tablecloth

Lesson

1. Introduce the title and author. Ask the students if they have seen flowers growing in their yards. Allow time for students to share.
2. Read the story and share the pictures.
3. Show the basket with the flowers and assist the students in sequencing the events in the story.

Closure: Dismiss students to check out.

Lesson 2

Martha Says It with Flowers

By Susan Meddaugh

Meddaugh, Susan. *Martha Says It with Flowers.* Boston: Houghton Mifflin Harcourt, 2010.

Summary: Martha wants to do something special for Grandma Lucille for her birthday to prove that she is a caring dog. It sure is hard to come up with a great gift for a human.

Skills: Retelling

Grade Level: First Grade

Materials: Pieces of colored construction paper
              Black marker, glue, and scissors

Instructions: Create three large flowers of different colors and styles and write "beginning," "middle," and "end" one on each of the flowers.

Lesson

1. Ask the students: Thumbs up if you have a dog at your house. Does he ever do things that get him or her into trouble? Give time for students to comment on their pets.
2. Explain that we are reading a story about Martha, who does wrong things sometimes. Read the book and share the pictures.
3. Review with the students the reason why Maratha wanted to do something special for Grandmom Lucille's birthday.

Closure: Lay out the three flowers labeled "beginning," "middle," and "end." Ask a student to retell what happened at the beginning of the story. If he needs help, call on a friend to help out. Move through the retelling by using the three flowers as prompts. Dismiss students to check out.

ZOO LESSONS

Lesson 3

Where's Walrus?

By Stephen Savage

Savage, Stephen. *Where's Walrus?* New York: Scholastic Press, 2011.

Summary: A walrus escapes from the zoo and hides in all kinds of places. The zookeeper eventually captures the walrus. This is a wordless book that will delight everyone.

Skills: Using imagination

Grade Level: Kindergarten

Materials: Drawing paper
Crayons

Lesson

1. Ask students if they have ever been to the zoo or seen wild animals? Allow time for students to share.
2. Introduce the title and author and tell the students that this is a wordless book. Ask them if they know what a wordless book is. Allow time for students to respond. If students don't know what a wordless book is, explain to them what wordless means. Tell the students that we will have to use our imagination and tell the story by looking at the pictures.
3. Share the pictures and encourage students to tell the story. Ask the students questions about each page and help them engage in telling the story. Examples: Where is the Walrus? What is the walrus doing?
4. Allow time for students to share another place Walrus might hide if the book had one more page. While students are checking out their books, allow time for students to draw a picture of Walrus hiding from the zookeeper.

Closure: Gather students and share pictures.

Lesson 3

My Rhinoceros

By Jon Agee

Agee, Jon. *My Rhinoceros.* New York: Scholastic, 2011.

Summary: A boy bought a pet rhinoceros at an exotic pet store. The problem was that the rhinoceros would not do anything, like fetch something. The boy asked a rhinoceros expert to help him find out why the rhinoceros would not do anything. The expert told the boy that rhinoceros do only two things, pop balloons and poke holes in kites. The boy's rhinoceros popped balloons and poked holes in kites during a bank robbery. The boy discovered that his rhinoceros could fly, too.

Skills: Problem
Solution
Sequencing

Grade Level: First Grade

Materials: A Balloon pattern
Colorful construction paper
Yarn

Instructions: Make several balloons using the colorful construction paper. Write one event from the story on each balloon. Examples: The boy bought a rhinoceros. The rhinoceros was quiet and shy. The boy tried to play fetch with the rhinoceros. The boy asked a rhinoceros expert to help him. Laminate the balloons and attach a piece of yarn to each balloon.

Lesson

1. Introduce the title and author. Tell the students that the boy in the story has a problem. Ask the students to listen to the story and talk to you about the problem and solution at the end of the story.
2. Read the story and share the pictures. Discuss the problem and solution. Problem: The boy's rhinoceros would not do anything. Solution: The rhinoceros expert told the boy what rhinoceroses were supposed to do, and the rhinoceros helped out with a bank robbery.

Closure: Show the balloons with the events of the story. Ask the students to put the balloons in order. You can lay the balloons on the floor in front of the students. Dismiss students to check out.

Lesson 3

Mr. Peek and the Misunderstanding at the Zoo

By Kevin Waldron

Waldron, Kevin. *Mr. Peek and the Misunderstanding at the Zoo*. Sonerville, MA: Templar Books, 2008.

Summary: Mr. Peek works at the zoo and talks to himself as he works. The animals overhear what Mr. Peek said and thinks that he is talking about them. The things that Mr. Peek said about himself were not that nice. The animals are very upset and sad because of the things that Mr. Peek said.

Skills: Problem
          Solution

Grade Level: Second Grade

Lesson

1. Introduce the title and author and tell the students that this book is about the zoo.
2. Also tell the students that this book has several problems and solutions, so ask them to listen carefully to the story and be prepared to discuss after hearing the story. Ask students to look for a black cat and little boy as you read through the story.
3. Read the story, share the pictures, and ask students to point out the cat and the little boy.
4. Talk about the problems and solutions. Problems: Mr. Peek wears the wrong jacket to work. Mr. Peek's words upset the animals. Solutions: Mr. Peek's son realizes the jacket switch. Mr. Peek's words after the switch to the right jackets make the animals feel better.

Closure: Dismiss students to check out.

VACATION LESSONS

Lesson 4

Maisy Goes on Vacation

By Lucy Cousins

Cousins, Lucy. *Maisy Goes on Vacation*. London: Walker Books Ltd., 2010.

Summary: Maisy goes to the beach for her vacation. She travels by train with many of her friends. Maisy stays in a hotel room and enjoys the beach with all of the many exciting activities.

Skills: Connecting text to self

Grade Level: Kindergarten

Materials: Chart paper or wipe-off board
        Marker

Instructions: Write on the board, "I am going on vacation and I am going to_____."

Lesson

1. Introduce the title and the author. Ask the students if their family has started to plan a summer vacation. Let the students respond with a show of hands. Tell the students to think about where they are going or where they would like to go on vacation while listening to the story.
2. Read the story and share the pictures.
3. Draw the students' attention to the wipe-off board. Read the words on the board and tell the students that we are going to play a game. Explain to the class that everyone will have a turn to say the words on the board. They will also need to repeat what everyone else has said before them. You will need to write each student's response on the board because it will be hard for kindergarteners to remember 25 places and they will also need help reading the responses.

Closure: Dismiss students to check out.

Lesson 4

Ladybug Girl at the Beach

By David Soman and Jacky Davis

Soman, David and Jacky Davis. *Ladybug Girl at the Beach.* New York: Dial Books for Young Readers, 2010.

Summary: Lulu has never been to the beach, but she knows she will love it. When Lulu arrives, she discovers that the waves are huge and noisy. Will she be brave enough to get into the ocean? Ladybug Girl is brave enough to do anything.

Skills: Sequencing the story

Grade Level: First Grade

Materials: 4- or 5-inch paper squares and marker
               Plastic sand pail

Instructions: On each of the squares, print out something that Lulu does at the beach. These should include building a sand castle, kite flying, eating ice cream treats, walking on the beach, drawing pictures in the sand, and collecting shells. Place the squares in the pail for later in the lesson.

Lesson

1. Share the title and ask if anyone has been to the beach. Explain that this story is about Lulu, who is going to the beach for the first time.
2. Read the story and share the pictures.
3. Using the pail, let students come one at a time to pick a square and read the words on the card. After all have been read, see if the students can put them in order as they happened in the story.

Closure: Stress that Lulu was afraid of the water at first. Ask for examples of when students have been afraid to try something new while on vacation. Give time to share but give yourself time to wrap up the discussion and for students to check out.

Lesson 4

Mrs. Millie Goes to Philly!

By Judy Cox

Cox, Judy. *Mrs. Millie Goes to Philly!* Madison, Tarrytown, NY: Marshall Cavendish, 2008.

Summary: Mrs. Millie is silly and uses animal words when she can in place of regular words. She might tell the students to hold hens with their friend instead of holding hands. On a trip to Philly, the students love to guess what she really means as they travel to important sights in the city.

Skills: Exploring the 900s in the nonfiction

Grade Level: Second Grade

Materials: Red, white, and blue paper cut in 6-inch squares and a marker

Instructions: Label the cards with call numbers of books about states and country section of the 900s. Pick out ones that the kids might be familiar with like their home state and historical places around where they live. Since this book is about Philadelphia, include this in your list.

Lesson

1. Ask for a volunteer to come up and read the title and author of the book. Predict what the story will be about. Give time for students to raise hands and explain. Where would Philly be located? If they have not heard of Philadelphia, Pennsylvania, point out that this is where the liberty bell is located.
2. After reading the story, review with the students the places that the class visited in the city.

Closure: Move the group over to the 900s section of the nonfiction books. Have them sit on the floor around the shelves. Stress that the book for today was a fiction or made-up story, but there is a section in the library where we can read fact books about places we might want to visit or learn about. Take turns letting different students match up the call numbers on the cards with books on the shelves. If possible, help each student select a book to look through back at the story corner. Dismiss students to check out. Collect books and return them to the shelves after the students leave to return to class.

RESOURCES

Mother's Day

DeGroat, Diane. *Mother, You're the Best! (But Sister, You're a Pest!)*. New York: HarperCollins, 2008.

May, Eleanor. *The Best Mother's Day Ever*. New York: Kane Press, 2010.

Flowers

Broyles, Anne. *Priscilla and the Hollyhocks*. Watertown, MA: Charlesbridge, 2008.

Bunting, Eve. *Flower Garden*. New York: Harcourt, 1994.

Cole, Henry. *On Meadowview Street*. New York: Greenwillow Books, 2007.

Haughton, Chris. *Oh No, George!* Somerville, MA: Candlewick Press, 2012.

Meddaugh, Susan. *Martha Says It with Flowers*. Boston: Houghton Mifflin Harcourt, 2010.

Pfister, Marcus. *Ava's Poppy*. New York: North-South Books, 2012.

Yolen, Jane and Heidi E. Y. Stemple. *Pretty Princess Pig*. New York: Little Simon, 2011.

Vacation

Day, Alexandera. *Carl's Summer Vacation*. New York: Farra Straus Giroux, 2008.

Falconer, Ian. *Olivia Goes to Venice*. New York: Atheneum Books for Young Readers, 2010.

Frazee, Marla. *A Couple of Boys Have the Best Week Ever*. Orlando: Harcourt, 2008.

Growar, Mick and Rory Walker. *Dad's Van*. New York: Crabtree Publishing Co., 2008.

Hayes, Karel. *The Summer Visitors*. Kowloon, Hong Kong: Down East Books, 2011.

London, Jonathan. *Froggy Goes to Hawaii*. New York: Viking, 2011.

McPhail, David. *Pig Pig Returns*. Watertown, MA: Charlesbridge, 2011.

Reed, Lynn Rowe. *Roscoe and the Pelican Rescue*. New York: Holiday House, 2011.

Seven, John. *The Ocean Story*. North Mankato, MN: Picture Window Books, 2011.

Teague, Mark. *LaRue ACROSS America: Postcards from the Vacation*. New York: Blue Sky Press, 2011.

Zoo

Comden, Betty and Adolph Green. *What's New at the Zoo?* Maplewood, NJ: Blue Apple Books, 2011.

Hall, Michael. *My Heart Is Like a Zoo.* New York: Greenwillow Books, 2010.

Mandel, Peter. *Zoo Ah-choooo.* New York: Holiday House, 2012.

McPhail, David. *Pig Pig Meets the Lion.* Watertown, MA: Charlesbridge, 2012.

Pilkey, Dav. *The Dumb Bunnies Go to the Zoo.* New York: Blue Sky Press, 2009.

Redmond, E. S. *Felicity Floo Visits the Zoo.* Somerville, MA: Candlewick Press, 2010.

Sierra, Judy. *Zoozical.* New York: Alfred A. Knopf, 2011.

Urbanovic, Jackie. *Duck and Cover.* New York: HarperCollins, 2009.

INDEX

ABOUT THE AUTHORS

BRENDA S. COPELAND has been an elementary librarian for the past 16 years in the Palmyra School District, Palmyra, PA. She earned her master's degree in library science from Kutztown University, PA, and her bachelor's degree in elementary education at the University of Delaware, Newark, DE.

PATRICIA A. MESSNER has been an elementary media specialist for the past 24 years in the Lebanon City School District, Lebanon, OH. She earned her master's degree in education from Miami University, Oxford, OH, and her bachelor's degree in elementary education at Asbury College, Wilmore, KY.

Books written by these authors are *Linking Picture Books to Standards* (Libraries Unlimited, 2003), *Collaborative Library Lessons for the Primary Grades* (Libraries Unlimited, 2004), *Using Picture Books to Teach Language Arts Standards in Grades 3–5* (Libraries Unlimited, 2006), *A Year of Picture Books* (Libraries Unlimited, 2007), *Everyday Reading Incentives* (Libraries Unlimited, 2009), *School Library Spaces: Just the Basics* (Libraries Unlimited, 2011), and *School Library Management: Just the Basics* (Libraries Unlimited, 2012).